Praise for *Out There*

"An adventure memoir unlike any I've read: fiercely hopeful, quietly subversive, and unapologetically queer. I wish someone had given me a book like this when I was growing up."

—ROBERT MOOR, author of *On Trails: An Exploration*

"I love this story. Once I started reading, I couldn't stop. It pulled me right in. It's strong and emotional but not sappy. I can't recommend it enough."

—BOBBIE SCOPA, author of *Both Sides of the Fireline: Memoir of a Transgender Firefighter*

"Garland's literary voice is not only timely. It is also critical at a moment in history when equity is threatened at every turn. His poetic, heartfelt, and often difficult experiences drive home the need for understanding and allyship around the world. Garland's storytelling is brave, but more importantly he reminds us that resilience and belief in the human spirit are fundamental to progress."

—JOANNA CROSTON, author of *Mountaineering Women: Climbing through History*

"Garland's story of heartbreak, persecution, and trauma from serving under Don't Ask, Don't Tell is as relevant as ever, with today's LGBTQ+ troops again facing scrutiny or separation for their identities. His gorgeous prose is an important reminder of the lasting consequences of putting policy before people."

—EMILY STARBUCK GERSON, editor of *Modern Military Magazine*

"Bold and enlightening."

—BRETT POPPLEWELL, author of *Outsider: An Old Man, a Mountain, and the Search for a Hidden Past*

"*Out There* is the raw, courageous memoir of living openly as a gay man over varied inhospitable terrain, from the military to the firefighting world to wilderness expeditions. Garland's courage during bootcamp, or climbing mountains, or racing to emergency scenes is never in doubt, but you will truly hold your breath when reading about the bravest act of all—his own self-acceptance. *Out There* is the template for those of us who need inspiration to explore the most wild and beautiful place, our own authentic life."

—CAROLINE PAUL, author of *The Gutsy Girl: Escapes for Your Epic Life of Adventure*

"Garland's story beautifully illustrates how our shared outdoor spaces can offer us more than just a connection to nature or a place to unwind our bodies. These spaces also provide opportunities for introspection and self-discovery as we navigate our personal journeys."

—BECCA CAHALL, executive producer of the *Dirtbag Diaries* podcast

Out There

Out There

DISPATCHES FROM MY PERSONAL WILDERNESS

LANCE GARLAND

TERRA FIRMA BOOKS ∞ TRINITY UNIVERSITY PRESS
San Antonio, Texas

Terra Firma Books, an imprint of
Trinity University Press
San Antonio, Texas 78212

Cover design by Anne Boston
Book design by BookMatters, Berkeley
Author photo by Ben Tibbetts

ISBN 978-1-59534-325-3 paper
ISBN 978-1-59534-326-0 ebook

Versions of these essays appeared in *Outside, Backpacker, Orion, Parks Stewardship Forum,* the *Seattle Times, The Stranger, Hidden Compass, Cutbank, OutServe,* and *Dirtbag Diaries.* Some names and identifying details have been changed to protect the privacy of individuals.

Trinity University Press strives to produce its books using methods and materials in an environmentally sensitive manner. We favor working with manufacturers that practice sustainable management of all natural resources, produce paper using recycled stock, and manage forests with the best possible practices for people, biodiversity, and sustainability. The press is a member of the Green Press Initiative, a nonprofit program dedicated to supporting publishers in their efforts to reduce their impacts on endangered forests, climate change, and forest-dependent communities.

The paper used in this publication meets the minimum requirements of the American National Standard for Information Sciences—Permanence of Paper for Printed Library Materials, ansi 39.48–1992.

CIP data on file at the Library of Congress

29 28 27 26 25 | 5 4 3 2 1

For Oliver

To be yourself in a world
that is constantly trying
to make you something else
is the greatest accomplishment.

RALPH WALDO EMERSON

Contents

Underwater

Of all the places in the world where I could have come to terms with my sexuality, I chose to go to Navy SEAL training when I was nineteen. At the most important moment of coming to terms with my identity, I had subconsciously placed myself in the center of a barrage of attractive men, all barely clothed, in a pool where I was literally swimming in the very thing I wanted to get away from: my attraction to them.

A nightmare phantasmagoria of assassin swimmers surrounds me in the pool, clad in their underwater demolition team shorts. On the beach, sand sticks to their sweating muscles as they perform athletic feats. Flashes of their naked bodies in the showers taunt me, while I try not to look at them. If for a moment I give in to these temptations, I will be in danger. These assassins could kill me. I'm just a goofy gay kid under the façade of an aspiring SEAL, coming to terms with the fact that not only am I incapable of changing who I am, but the people around me are starting to notice.

Basic Underwater Demolitions School (BUD/S), Navy SEAL training, water competency drills: with hands held behind our backs and bands tied around our ankles, we prepare for First Phase, which consists of the notorious Hell Week. Our task today is to bob up and down in the pool, breathing out all the air in our lungs so we can sink to the bottom, then push off and glide back to the surface for a breath. Up and down, doing our best to stay calm and in control.

I've read a lot of books about the history of Navy SEALs, which stands for SEa, Air, and Land. John F. Kennedy created the SEALs in the early 1960s and recruited from the already legendary Underwater Demolitions Teams (UDTs), known as frogmen, an elite force of men that formed secretive amphibious assault teams. The SEALs were meant to take those elite waterborne teams and train them to assault from the air and on land. They would be a team unlike any other, capable of extreme precision in any environment, and meant to do so silently and without warning.

As a teenager, reading the books and watching the television shows, I dreamt of jumping out of airplanes into the sea, swimming to shore, and inserting into land-based targets. The action called to me, and when the 9/11 terrorist attacks happened, I had all the catalyst I needed to drive me here. I was extremely focused for my age and had trained methodically for more than three years to get to this pool, passing many tests and barriers on the way to get here, obstacles that filtered out many aspiring candidates. But the biggest obstacle was coming: the infamous Hell Week, just a month away.

I've been near the front of the pack in most disciplines here, so I feel confident and determined. I will become a frogman. But as I sink to the bottom of the pool and thrust myself back up to the surface, I'm reminded of when I was eleven, in my childhood pool, where I did the same thing for long periods. But I didn't think of myself as a frogman then; I thought of myself as a fish. More specifically, a merman. At the end of Disney's *The Little Mermaid*, an iconic figure captured my attention: King Triton, with his muscular upper body, his athletic fin, and the golden trident he powerfully wielded. I wanted to be like him; there was something about him that I felt akin to, as if we were somehow similar.

One day in that pool, as I'm swimming around with my legs together, formed in one big fin, I notice something that draws every bit of my attention. There, outside the pool, stands a teenage boy with some chest hair and toned muscles. His board shorts cling tightly to his body, and underneath, something I haven't seen before. It's like mine, but so much bigger. He repositions it to make it less obvious, but that doesn't help. My mouth agape, I push farther into the deep side of the pool, my eyes just above the ripples, transfixed by the teenager in his wet shorts.

He strides about like a show horse, flaunting his beauty to the most popular teenage girl in the neighborhood. She postures on the other side of the chain-link fence, both leaning into each other. His hands are over his head, fingers in between the links, body extending into a larger form as she leans lower into his. Her chest lifts upward.

I imagine myself in the place of this teen girl, desiring of his attention. What would it feel like if he looked at me that way, if he leaned over me, made me feel like no one else around matters? I know this one thing: I'm drawn to him. It's simple.

The boy turns to jump into the pool and momentarily spots my gaze. I slip beneath the water before he surfaces to confront me. My lungs burn as I swim as far away as I can with that short breath.

Here in this pool full of Navy SEAL candidates, I know I'm not like the young men who resemble tadpoles, forming limbs and turning into frogmen. I'm going through a completely different metamorphosis. I feel like a hatchling fish, with no mouth and no way to feed myself other than by devouring my own body. I desperately want to turn into a tadpole, but instead I'm turning into a young fish fry, and I must become capable of feeding myself or I won't survive. I'm morphing into a creature different than the boys in this pool. And they're starting to notice.

A few days ago, fellow candidates and I went rock climbing and bouldering in the mountains near San Diego. Jake, a man in his thirties whom I want to emulate, tells stories of climbing, sailing, and adventuring around the globe. That is the life I want, and I'm enthralled with him. In moments of enthusiasm, moments when I lose my bearing and reveal my true self, my voice gets higher and loose. At that precise moment of my revealed enthusiasm, one of the other guys asks me, "Why are you so gay?" I don't say anything, I just freeze, like I've been stunned by a punch. It isn't a question out of curiosity—it's a condemnation, a slur. I have no words to respond. We keep climbing.

Back in the pool, I wrestle with this question. *Why am I so gay?* The question sends me reeling with anxiety. Jake recommended a book for me to read, Jon Krakauer's *Into the Wild*, and I immediately have a strong connection with the protagonist, Alexander Supertramp. I relate to how he completely gave up on society. If I accept myself, I will inevitably be shunned and embark upon the same journey he did. The bus that he lived and died in is symbolic for me and represents my greatest fear: being an outcast. From my vantage point, I see no place in society for a guy like me. That's part of why I came here, attempting to overcome this part of my identity, as if SEAL training is some sort of conversion camp.

But I can't shake this no matter how hard I try.

Here I am underwater again. I've always been like this. With all these men around me, I can't help but look at the beautiful ones. We all wear khaki-colored UDT shorts that resemble Daisy Duke cutoffs. A few of the candidates don't wear underwear, revealing everything underneath. Why did I think that coming here would fix me? It's comical that I thought this could be the answer, being immersed in men.

My father suspected. Before the start of my enlistment in the Navy, as I left the house for my job as a security guard, he waited for me outside.

"Are you gay?" he asked, his voice both alarmed and confused.

I stared at him, unwilling and unable to understand the question.

He waited for a beat. "I found something in your car while I cleaned it," he said, and pulled out a muscle magazine. He fanned it open, revealing chiseled men in translucent briefs, then slapped it shut.

I lunged for the magazine and took it with force. "You can't go through my things!"

"The military is going to do more than that," he said. A wave of fear traveled with his voice.

It had been one thing to fly under the radar and just pretend, but it was a whole other thing to be confronted about who I am. When people ask me straight out if I'm gay, I don't want to lie. I don't want to pretend, even though I hate myself for it.

On weekend leave a few days ago, my buddies and I went to the mall in San Diego to get some R&R. I went to grab some frozen yogurt with one of the guys while the rest of the crew went to get burgers at the other end of the food court. My buddy said he needed to buy something, so I sat alone. The perfect embodiment of the California surfer walked up to me.

"Hey, dude." His blond hair contrasted with the depth of his tan. He had perfect white teeth.

"Hey," I said.

His smile set me at ease. "How's it going?" He got a bit closer as he talked. He was warm and friendly, an athlete in incredible shape. His shirt set on his body like a jersey on a football player's shoulder pads.

"Not bad, just hanging with some friends." I looked around for them. The surfer didn't look away from me. "What about you?" I said.

"Just chilling. I saw you from across the way. Couldn't keep my eyes off you. Damn, dude, you're hot."

I was so flattered I didn't know what to say. I felt the urge to kiss him. My stomach churned. This was the first time a man had ever hit on me, and a guy of his caliber was beyond my daydreams. I got lost in his blue eyes and felt a little lightheaded. Then the alarm bells started going off. I looked around for my friends. Were they watching this? Shit.

"Can I take you out to dinner, bro?" the guy said, getting closer to me. He was about to put his arm around my shoulder.

I backed away.

"It's okay, dude, I know you want it. I want you too."

Too far, too fast. Something was not right. Alarm bells kept ringing. I backed away without a word, walked fast, until I could see my cohort standing in a group on the other side of the court. They were laughing among themselves. I walked up and stood outside the circle, not sure what they were laughing about. I didn't say anything. I was trying desperately to figure out what had just happened.

"What happened to you?" one of the guys says. "You look like you've seen a ghost." He snickered and put his hand on my shoulder.

At that moment, the mystery man, the surfer with the tan and the perfect teeth, walked toward the group. Shit! What would I say? This was not good. How would I explain this?

He got closer, and one of my friends in the group said, "I want you to meet my friend, Nate."

Totally confused, I had no words. His friend? Why on earth would his friend want to take me out to dinner and say all those things? Accepting an invitation like that could be enough to get me kicked out of the military.

Nate reached his hand out to mine, grabbed it, and shook it. "Nice to meet you." He smiled, came to my side, and put his arm around my shoulder. He pulled me into his huge chest and his slightly musty odor.

"See, I told you he's not gay!" said Brian, a friend from boot camp, as if repeating it for the umpteenth time.

The group laughed again, but I still didn't get it. Didn't say anything. Nate kept his arm around me, as if in some strange form of protection. He was still smiling. Looking deeply at me. Warmly.

"I asked Nate to hit on you. Had to make sure you weren't gay, bro."

"It's because you're so fucking gay."

"He's not gay, dude, he's from Seattle. It's just how they are," Brian said.

"It's cool, bro, I got you." Nate squeezed me into him. The warm dampness of his armpit was like a cave I wanted to recede into. I didn't say a word.

And then there was that night recently. I was in the back seat with two of my fellow candidates, driving aimlessly around San Diego because the rest of the guys were out at the bars and we were underage. One of the guys in the front seat suggested that we go to Hillcrest, the gay area, and drive around looking for a gay guy to harass. I was mortified, unsure of what he was planning, but I remained silent. It didn't take long for us to get there. The guy in the front passenger seat noticed a guy walking by himself and told the driver to let him out a block away. We drove by as we watched him walk up to the stranger. The driver circled the block, and when we returned they were gone. The driver got worried. He sped around the block again and then started driving up and down different streets. After a long while, our guy reappeared out of an alley, alone and in a frenzy. We picked him up and he told us to get out of there. The driver questioned him, asked what happened. He said that the guy was fucking crazy, half out of breath, sweaty and slightly disheveled. But he had done something. Did he beat up the guy? I look at his hands and don't see any blood. There are no marks or cuts on his skin. Something gave me the impression that he had messed around with the stranger in the alley. But I didn't say anything. Either way, this was dangerous and not to be discussed further. We were in taboo territory, so we sped away from Hillcrest and back to the beach.

As I bob up and down in the pool, I look over to the two guys I had been in the car with that night. They look unaffected and focused on the task at hand. The one who disappeared that night is a handsome specimen of an athlete. His ripped abs flex as he pushes himself to the surface. Could he have had sex with the stranger that night? I can barely imagine it. It's far more possible that he beat the guy in a violent hate crime. A deeper question surfaces for me: If I were in the position to have sex with that stranger, would I?

In the large gang-style shower the other day, all these beautiful naked men in front of me, I focused on not looking at anything or anyone. The showers here are the scariest place I've ever been, and I know that one tiny slip will be my end. There is nowhere to hide. There are showerheads a foot apart on three walls, about twenty of them. As the first twenty men shower, the rest must wait in line for our turn. At a certain point in the line, you must hang your towel on a hook, move forward, and stand there naked until a showerhead opens. I'm standing at the front of the line, my hands clasped in front of me covering my nakedness, as uncomfortable as ever. A handsome friend finishes his shower and comes up in front of me, perfectly comfortable being naked and seen. He looks me straight in the eye and swings his manhood around in circles with his hips, laughing and taunting me. He watches my eyes lower to look at him as he swings it around, and he proudly smiles, gets closer. I remember how I yearned for the teen's attention in the pool all those years ago. Now I have this beautiful man's attention. His body inches away from mine, naked and fully open. A moment of pure excitement, my body reacts to his, it says everything that my words and thoughts cannot. That fleeting instant is followed by dread and panic. I run to the showerhead, turn it cold, and drown my head in the frigid water.

Back in the pool during water competency training, I'm underwater, silent and safe. Can I allow myself to finish that moment in the shower? What happens if I dream of being with him, of becoming the first openly gay Navy SEALs together? For the first time, I accept the daydream. I've experienced the horror of being here as a nightmare phantasmagoria of mortal danger, but as I accept the gravitational pull of my daydream, the experience of being here in this moment morphs into a synchronized swimming montage where I embrace, for an underwater moment, gay joy. I imagine the guy from the shower and me in the center of this glorious group of half-naked men, fully supported and part of the group, like the band of three hundred Theban warriors of ancient Greece, in a time where we could be warrior lovers. I sink down to the bottom of the pool and half-smile at the thought. Why should I loathe myself for this thing that I cannot change? Though I've become comfortable underwater, my whole existence forged by this pressure, I'm tired of pretending. Is there something more out there, a place where I can exist as something other than this submerged creature, a hatchling fish without a mouth in danger of being eaten by frogs? What's wrong with being a fish-man anyway? Triton was the son of Poseidon and god of the depths of the sea. He wrestled with heroic figures and commanded the waves with his conch shell. Although our current culture might view a merman as an inferior cartoon character, in a different time, mermen were revered in mythology.

In this huge Olympic-size pool, surrounded by the muscular bodies of all these dedicated men who sink and bob in columns of uniform determination, I dream of a place in my current time in history, where someone like me can come up for air.

Surf Torture

The compound was located just south of the Hotel del Coronado in San Diego. At the entrance a three-foot wooden sign stood on two posts. The wood was weathered with worn, rounded edges; engraved deep in the wood were the words "Naval Special Warfare Center: Basic Underwater Demolitions / SEAL Training Facility" in yellow paint that peeled and flaked in the warm night breeze. Just past the sign and on the left was a small guard shack with an armed sentry inside. The entrance led into a large concrete square surrounded by concrete buildings on all sides. Drawn into the long-since dried pavement was the title "The Grinder," and above it, mounted to the headquarters building, was an expertly polished bell that gleamed under a lucid moon. Directly ahead of the bell was a three-story barracks that housed the aspiring warriors, to the right was a two-story building with large white lettering above the front door that read "Medical," and to the left was an indoor diving facility four stories high. There were only two ways in or out of the Grinder: the entrance with an armed sentry or the small alley to the left of the barracks. The alley led to an obstruction: a man-made sand dune that rose steeply, then fell to the sea.

First Phase. Day three. I jerk awake to the sound of explosions, swing my feet over the side of the bunk, and jump to the cold floor. There is a clamor in the hall. I grab my camouflage pants and pull them over my black spandex shorts. Clasp the belt tight. The white stenciled T-shirt with my last name on the chest sticks to my already sweating skin as I pull it on. It's dark, but my eyes start to adjust. I grab my combat boots and shove them on my feet, carefully place my pile of gear in order across my perfectly trim bed: combat knife sharpened to perfection, inflatable life preserver with fresh CO_2 cartridge, one expertly painted combat helmet in green drab and stickered with my name, Garland, and class number, 252, on it. Just as I grab my camo jacket, a blinding wave of light and sound devours the room.

A horde of barking voices scream, "Drop!"

I do just that. Out of the corner of my eye I see them, clad in worn camouflage pants and blue T-shirts with the golden SEAL trident on the left breast. They are eight strong and surround us.

"Push 'em out!"

I crank out twenty push-ups and attempt to center my mind in the chaos.

The four of us yell, "Hooyah!"

We do hundreds of push-ups in sets of twenty while they growl at us from above, then push us with our gear out the door and into a hallway clogged with pedestrian traffic. Bodies are everywhere. The instructors do not tire. Down three flights of stairs and into a gauntlet of pressurized water, we crawl and come out into the Grinder. They keep the hoses on us. Water burns my eyes as I see flares igniting the courtyard on all sides. Explosions come from the corners as they line us up in ranks.

"Time for inspection! At-ten-tion!"

I jump erect and hurriedly adjust my knife, life preserver, and helmet. We are in disarray. Everyone fails.

"Hit the surf. Wet and sandy!"

In an instant three hundred men push through the small alley and hit the sand dune. The grit sticks to me like tar as I struggle to climb to the top, then run down toward the sea with the fury of a raging battalion of soldiers. A crashing assault of bodies collides with the ocean. We crawl out and run back to the dune, dive into the coarse sand, and cover every crevice of our bodies with it. We roll in it, then climb back up and over. The Grinder greets us with gushing hoses. The sand cuts our skin.

Once back into ranks, the instructors yell, "Drop!"

Apparently we aren't sandy enough. They send us out to the surf again and again. I lose track of time.

I've been working hard for years to get here. The frigid waters of Puget Sound could have given me hypothermia in minutes, but I didn't care. At seventeen years old, I was training for a goal, and the cold water gave me a rush, plus the promise of escape. Some days, my swim buddy couldn't make it, but I swam anyway. If my mother knew I was alone, she'd skin me alive, but I needed to train, so I did. Today the marine fog has settled like night across the expanse. I can't see very far in front of me. I stick as close to the shore as possible, and when my hands touch the rocky seabed, scratching the tips of my fingers, I push myself farther out of sight from the shore.

I've been swimming out here in a short-sleeved, short-pant wetsuit designed primarily for surfers in California rather than the cold waters of Washington. I'm ill-equipped for this training, much less for the training to come, and today I can barely see ahead. With my buddy Carl, who was training with me to become a SEAL, I have swum offshore every major beach in the Seattle suburban area, climbing out of the water to eat blackberries from wild bushes and jumping back in again to swim miles of coastline.

Today I'm swimming out my demons. Things have gone too far lately. I try to forget about it, but a few days ago I hit on a guy. I asked him out on a date, out to dinner no less. I'd been talking to a painter, Brian, while at work at my security guard job for weeks. He'd been doing a project for my company and was always eager to get into conversation with me. His tight khaki pants and paint-speckled hands attracted me. Deep in conversation, looking into his translucent blue eyes, I breached the gap.

"Want to get dinner sometime before I leave for the Navy?"

His radiant smile started to blink out and then regained its full charge. He was mulling it over, as if it were a game of one-on-one basketball, a game I couldn't beat him at.

"That would be great, bro, but we're going to have to bring our girlfriends. Is that okay?" He kept smiling, but his words were toeing a line.

"Oh, yeah, definitely dude, of course, no problem." Stop talking, Lance. It's painfully obvious that I'm painfully obvious.

"You have a girlfriend?" he asked in the nicest, most incredulous way possible.

"Yes. Yes, I do," I said. My forehead started to sweat.

"Okay, buddy," he said, and put his hand on my shoulder. I relaxed into his touch. "I'll ask her when's a good time and get back to you." There was a twinkle in his eye like a wink, amusement at my expense but also an apology.

I swim harder and faster. How could I have been so dumb? Of course he's straight. What was I thinking? At least he gave me a way out. But I'm not gay. I'm. Not. Gay. Nothing happened. Just keep swimming.

My thoughts take me places I don't want to go. That's the problem with swimming—all you have is you.

Growing up, my family didn't have much money. When I was fourteen, my parents homeschooled my siblings and me for a year in order to control the influence of the outside world on us. Our church espoused the importance of a private education, away from the temptations of secular life, but since my father had just lost his last job—due to a failed drug test—we didn't have the money to pay for the Christian school tuition. Homeschooling was my parents' last option. My father got the family a paper route, which my brother Jude and I ran on weekday afternoons and the whole family managed in the early-morning hours on weekends. The paper route didn't last long, and my mom got a job as a maid to allow us time to do our studies.

Part of the program was to visit other homeschooled kids, and one of those families had a boy a year older than me. He was the athletic type: blue-eyed, blond, and already showing signs of toned muscle. He mentioned to me one day that he had kissed a boy, and he was proud. I was enthralled with him and wished he would kiss me, even though that thought instilled great blooms of shame within me. Somehow he was everything I wanted to be but couldn't allow myself to become. And then one day his secret was made visible. My mother was concerned. The whole community was. He was sent to a conversion camp. The last time I saw him before he left, he had lost all his verve. He was pale, afraid, and he was changed. He became a cautionary tale. Never, under any circumstance, tell anyone who I really am.

A few weeks ago, during the Indoctrination Phase of training, the instructors told us that the U.S. Olympic team had just been here. Next month the 2004 Olympics in Athens were set to begin, and the athletes came here for some final inspiration from the greatest warriors on earth. The instructors told us that the most important knowledge they could share with the Olympians was that they were capable of more than they believed they were. People can move far past their own understanding of their abilities. Like the candidates who fight to attend this most elite of military schools and make it through the arduous training, the Olympians could push past their boundaries and become something far greater than their minds could comprehend.

That was the curriculum here. To push past every boundary of self, to rise above the torture and pain, and to transcend, even spiritually, the physical limitations of our belief. To confirm this possibility, we sat through lectures about the greatest athletes in history. We learned about how Buddhist monks overcame environmental conditions to sit naked on the tops of ice-covered mountains. We were told to read Victor Frankl's book *Man's Search for Meaning*, which I read immediately. I understood the vital importance of what they were trying to teach us here. We could persevere through anything. This training was meant to break us, and only those who could persevere would survive it.

Frankl was proof of that. He survived the Holocaust, but his family members—his father Gabriel, mother Elsa, wife Tilly, and brother Walter—were murdered in the Auschwitz, Bergen-Belsen, and Theresienstadt concentration camps. Somehow he survived despite the horror, and from this terror he created a new form of psychotherapy that helped countless individuals overcome daunting psychological conditions. His theories revolved around "tragic optimism," which overcomes what he called the "tragic triad," which consists of pain, guilt, and death. This tragic optimism can be maintained by finding meaning in our lives. When asked how we find meaning, he explained, "All we can do is study the lives of people who seem to have found their answers to the questions of what ultimately human life is about." Our SEAL instructors were giving us examples of people who had found meaning in life, because they knew that the main battle of this training program was not being fought by us physically, though it was clearly breaking down our bodies; the main battle was being fought in our minds.

"Log PT!" the instructors scream.

We crawl out of the sea, and to our left are rows of enormous logs. I try to regain control of my breath. The log is hard to hold, almost slippery. My biceps pull it to my chest, trying to get the timing perfect so that my team of six can lift it in one fluid move. We curl it, hold it to our chest and do sit-ups with it, throw it over our heads and catch it, and run up and down the beach with it raised high. They make us do squats as my muscles howl with agony. My mind stops. For a long time I'm unsure of anything. A haze flows over me like a dark tapestry. My pulse beats, thump—thump—thump.

With the log in my arms, I realize that my body is still working. How on earth can it work without my mind? It doesn't feel possible that I'm still doing the work my body experiences. There's a complete disconnection between my mind and body. My arms have taken over. They are stronger than my mind. An immense calm covers everything. My scope of reality draws in on the movements of muscle and wood. I watch in awe. I must learn to break this boundary in reverse, have my brain tell my body it can do things it doesn't believe possible. Or at the very least, my mind must keep up.

We drop the trunks, run three miles to inhale our lunch, and run three miles back. Men puke while we run. I'm one of them. I take a swig from my canteen and spit it out after flushing my mouth.

The instructors decide it's time for some "boat races."

Standing more than six-foot-three, I was originally placed in a boat crew that consisted of the tallest men in the class. But just three days into this phase there are only two of us left, so we're put into a boat crew of much shorter men. The inflatable boats weigh two hundred pounds, and we carry them on our heads as we race around the beach. Because of our height difference, the boat barely rests on the shorter men's heads and is unevenly on our two taller heads. It crashes disjointedly back and forth as it wobbles and jerks, trying to find the heads of the shorter men. Pain stabs my neck like a jackhammer. The boat rubs the top of my shaved head raw and bloody. I try to squat and run, attempting to even out the load with the rest of the boat crew.

The class leader, an enlisted candidate who had previously washed out and returned to try his luck again, runs up from behind us and screams, "Hey, boat crew, Garland is a shit bag and isn't carrying his load!"

He runs off screaming profanities at me as I try to straighten my back and neck to take the full load. The fury in me wells up. How could he treat me like that. I watched him on national television as he cried and quit. He was a major character in the Discovery channel documentary series, and I remember feeling such empathy for him. Now I'm here with him, and he's trying to eat us alive. We have enough of that from the instructors.

The instructors scream, "Thirteen Stages of Hell!"

It's a competition. As the SEALs say, "It pays to be a winner." There is one winner in each phase, and if you win you get a break to watch the next race. The stages consist of various physical feats. I don't win any.

Hell is a concept I'm intimately acquainted with. This torture is no different from how I've been raised. I think back to mission's week. The ground behind our doublewide-trailer-turned-church has been broken. Our congregation doesn't have the money to build the new facility, so that is the reason to have all these visiting missionaries and evangelists come for a weeklong festival of fire-and-brimstone gospel, along with a measured dose of brotherly love.

I sit in the third pew back on the left, the area where the teen group amasses, and watch slideshows of missionaries in far-off lands doing the Lord's work of bringing running water and salvation to the inhabitants of godless places. There is a sense of humanity that reaches me through the pictures, a sense of wonder and of connection that inspires me to daydream of doing the same work. My parents have always encouraged us to be missionaries. The walls of our home are filled with pictures of unfortunate children in places where they have little or no opportunity to thrive. Our dad has always said, "What about the starving kids in Ethiopia?" That's his response to any problem or misgiving we have about life. A sense of humanitarianism was in our hearts from a very young age; in fact, that is the only job we've been groomed for.

The next speaker gets up to the pulpit, and the tone of the room shifts from loving and compassionate to angry and sinister. I sit next to my best friend, Jeremiah, who is seventeen, a year older than me. He quietly chuckles at the red-faced man who waddles up to the podium. I push my leg up against his to silence his outburst and leave it there. A strict rule in church: all teens of the opposite sex must keep a Bible between them to keep temptation at bay. Who knows what could happen if two people of the opposite sex touch each other in service? Virginity is of the utmost importance. Ironically, they never think to say two people of the same sex can't touch, so even as I sit next to my best friend, feeling the warmth of his body, I don't acknowledge the contradiction yet. When I was a kid playing tag with the neighborhood children, I stated, quite assuredly, "Girls can't touch me, only boys!"—a statement that followed me as a joke throughout my childhood.

"God hates homosexuals. They are an abomination and are condemned to hell!" the man spouts and spits with fervor.

I come back from my daydream and sit up straight at attention. The man continues his rant, his tirade against sin. Our regular pastor does his best to keep things positive, but as a whole homosexuality is well known to be the worst of all sins. As I sit in the pew, the warmth between my best friend's leg and mine causes me to sweat profusely. I pull away. Flashes of images of Jeremiah and me run through my brain: shirtless on the barn roof, exercises in nothing but gym shorts, touching each other's muscles, full nakedness, masturbation in front of each other, sleeping side by side, cuddling. The list of sins runs through my brain. I'm paranoid that the entire congregation knows what I'm thinking, as if it's projected on the back of my head like the slideshows the missionaries used moments before. I sweat thick beads of guilt that run down my forehead as the evangelist bellows and condemns that and other sins. This is nothing new. It has been happening since I was a child, and I know what to do. Confess to God all of my sins, ask for forgiveness. Profess that I will never think such thoughts again. Before long, my repetitious prayers bring an end to the tirade. The evangelist says to go before the altar and ask for forgiveness from Almighty God, so I slump to the front with my shoulders curled in toward my chest. On my knees I beg, implore God, to be changed, to be absolved from my sin. Somewhere deep inside me I come to a resolution that everyone in the congregation has the same thoughts and feelings as me, and that I am not so very different. What matters is to not act on such desires. What matters is to ask for forgiveness. I rise, the service ends, and I walk out of the auditorium with the rest of the sinners.

After the service, the group of teenagers goes to a 9/11 rally. We've been going to these rallies for weeks, ever since it happened. On the main drag people line the streets like the Fourth of July, flags everywhere, streamers and sparklers and hats and other patriotic swag. People cheer. Music blares. A parade of people walks down the closed-off street and rallies the onlookers.

I've been distancing myself from Jeremiah, who has started dating my sister. Things have been tense after the last time we spent the night together, since I put my hands on him in a moment of passion, since I crossed that line, and he allowed it but did not reciprocate. My self-loathing truly marred our friendship. He's tried everything to reconnect, but I am in crisis mode and working on damage control.

In the flurry of patriotic fervor, I watch Jeremiah wrap his arm around my sister. Still sweating from the service beforehand, angry about the 9/11 attacks and so much more, feeling a sense of duty to my country, a sense of duty to God, and realizing that there is no way in hell that I can possibly have these horrible desires if I were to go to the manliest place on the planet, I decide under the red, white, and blue haze of that parade to join the U.S. Navy and become a Navy SEAL. That will fix everything.

Back at SEAL training, I reach the seventh stage of hell, and they call off the evolution because most candidates have finished the stages already. I'm not used to being in the back of the pack, but I'm fighting more than just this training right now. There is a battle going on in my mind, and I can barely see through the fog of it. I realize that in many ways, I've volunteered for self-imposed conversion therapy by coming here. My motivations have become clear in this torturous place. This is all a cover-up, a last-ditch attempt to hold onto the teachings of my youth. The problem is, I no longer believe in those teachings.

We're thirteen miles away from headquarters and must run back. Pain is now my name. I'm at the back of the pack, and the instructors make the leaders run behind to motivate us stragglers. My right knee is locked, and my vision is blurry. A lot of guys are quitting.

Relief washes over my spine when the instructors scream, "Surf Torture!"

Their screaming doesn't affect me as much as I anticipated. I've joked with my fellow candidates that no one can yell at me like my father did. It's true. I've spent the past eighteen years in his household—his lectures would last for hours, punctuated by his screaming voice whenever I challenged his authority, which I calmly did on a regular basis. It wasn't that I had a problem with authority; I couldn't be in the Navy, much less be here, if I did. I had a problem with things not making sense. Where I'm at in the world right now, none of this, not my childhood religion, not the basis of my family, not my reason for being here, nothing makes any sense.

We run into the waves and lock arms. The nefarious cold takes hold. I interlace my fingers, holding them tight over my chest in an effort to keep my elbows locked into the arms of the men at my sides. We are one large chain of men laid out to rust in the sea. In the dark of that cold torture, my thoughts wander. All I can think of is the phone call four days ago. My parents picked a good time to get a divorce. I guess it didn't make sense to them either. Afterward my father tried to kill himself and was hospitalized. Once I left home, the world I knew completely imploded. My family needs me, and I'm not there for them. My current quest seems unimportant in comparison. But there is no good solution. I'm losing something no matter where I turn.

The waves crash over our heads. Instructors on the beach are too far away to be heard. The men at my sides cling to me, shivering in focus and silent determination.

Here I lie, immersed in the destruction of my life. Alone, family fractured, keenly aware of my difference among the most elite of heterosexual men, nearly smoked out by them that day at the mall, and now the class leader has turned on me. I thrash amid the chaos of life, knowing there is no future here for a man like me. As an irregular link in this great chain of men, the all-consuming pain takes hold. Few choices remain: to stay in this place where I do not fit, or to ring the bell and go forth.

All the things I've been learning here are having an unexpected effect on me. For all the boundary-pushing, breaking, and moving past our own understanding, the knowledge shared by these SEALs is opening a door to something I didn't think I could do, something I didn't think I could be, far past the boundaries of what my childhood education has prepared me for.

I think of Victor Frankl, of his time in the concentration camps and the wisdom he was able to wring out of the terror of life. What could I make of my own terror? What could add meaning to my forsaken life? His admonition, "Say yes to life in spite of everything," echoes in my mind with the waves crashing over me. "Life is potentially meaningful under any conditions, even those which are most miserable. And this in turn presupposes the human capacity to creatively turn life's negative aspects into something positive or constructive."

I thought coming here would turn me into a SEAL. Instead, it's giving me the ability to turn into something else.

In the violent stillness of surf torture, my inner compass takes a strong bearing. I will not stay here. I will find a home where I can be free. That truth crashes fearfully upon me. I silently weep in the surf. This place is the last remnant of my former self. When I quit, I will lose everything that is behind me. There will be no going back. This is a boundary that will transform me forever.

Shivers set in, the shaking foundational, in the core of my being. I hold onto the men beside me in an effort to not dissipate in the dark. A nauseous quake forms inside me, the death of a history, a great breakdown. The waves crash.

I allow my fingers to slip. A link in that chain of men washes away.

Washed Out to Sea

On the weather decks of my naval warship, in the wilderness of the Pacific Ocean, I smoked alone. It was my second deployment, my first without Easy.

Very little signified time's passing, save for sunsets and cigarettes. Cigarettes like scratch marks on prison walls to count the days, scars on the walls of my lungs. We didn't get breaks for their own sake, but I found a loophole: the weather deck, where the habit could buy you a few minutes of rest.

In my smoking reverie, fellow sailors would come to me with words of apprehension.

"They've started an investigation."

"They're monitoring your email."

"You need to cover your ass."

"Tell everyone it's not true."

"You can't possibly win."

"You know what's coming."

Over the course of the first few weeks of our six-month deployment, faces from the 250-man crew sifted before me like a kaleidoscope of melancholy colors. Nauseated and dizzy from the onslaught, I inhaled one cigarette after another, leaned against the side irons, and trained my gaze on the gray sea. I couldn't possibly know how to respond, but most of them weren't there to listen anyway. They were characters in a drama, all playing their roles.

A southern man and his two friends stared murderously at me, like wolves stalking a weak member of the herd, waiting to strike. They were friends of the accused man, and as I averted my eyes and looked toward the thrashing sea below the ship, I imagined his threats against me coming to life. Perhaps one of them would collide with me as I walked the long gangway down the exterior of the ship. A dark figure would push me into the lifelines—the retractable railings that were lowered for gun shoots—and they would shake with my body against them, whitecapped waves roiling below me like shark teeth.

"If someone were to fall out here," he had told me, "they wouldn't be found."

There were few things I could hold onto during this period of my life, amid the chaos of faces, information, and uncertainty, and those things composed what truth I could cobble together at any given point. The truth about myself, who I was, and what happened to Easy. But one night, as I smoked and mused about the state of feeling lost at sea, a spectacle revealed itself in the waters before me. All around, from every vantage point I could see, lights rose out from the depths of the ocean. These clusters of bioluminescence glowed with neon green-and-blue sparks, rising from the deep as exploding universes. The water radiated with those solar systems, galaxies of glowing life. The cloudless sky reflected the phosphorescent emissions of light as the stars of the empyrean inverted from the nebula-like clusters rising from the sea. I sat between all the splendor and felt the utter insignificance of my existence, and somehow this signal from the sea made me feel less alone.

About a year and a half earlier—not long before I left for my first six-month deployment—I came out to my family before my twentieth birthday. My mom was in shock and could not speak to me. My siblings were confused but supportive, and unexpectedly my father simply told me that he loved me. A few weeks later at my grandfather's funeral, a former Navy man himself, I wore my dress-blues uniform to honor his service at the veterans' memorial cemetery. Stuck together in the car on the hours-long ride home, my father confronted me in front of the family and told me I was going to hell, that I was an abomination to God. I told him I didn't believe it. Soon after, I left for Southeast Asia aboard my naval warship. My mother didn't speak to me for six months. It was a scandal, and I was the cause of it.

On the day that I was given an introductory tour of my Navy ship, the USS *Rodney M. Davis*, and my new job as gunner's mate, I crossed paths with a swaggering boatswain's mate who held the coveted bosun's pipe. He was a second-class petty officer, the second-in-command of my new ship's boatswain department, with a joker's smile and a few teeth capped in silver. The bosun's pipe was a whistle, but more so it was a symbol of power, and with its trill he could command his crew of seaman to do his bidding. His nickname was Easy, short for Ezekiel.

On our first port of call, the shores of Okinawa, our eyes wouldn't stop meeting. We were soon inseparable, in large part because I'd taken up smoking. We'd light each other's cigarettes with our own, daring, when no one else was around, to keep the cigarettes in our mouths the whole time, our heads leaned toward each other, the tips kissing.

In the luxurious foyer of a four-star Singapore hotel, he told me he would reserve a room if I stood guard by the front door. I sat in the air-conditioned lounge, trying to dry the thick sweat from my body, and I watched Easy out of the corner of my eye. My nerves were like lightning. I had no idea what I would say if we got caught. I hadn't been granted overnight privileges, and we had to be back to the ship by 2000 hours. There was no reason why we would be spending four hundred dollars on a hotel room we'd only use for a few hours.

As Easy was finishing the paperwork, the only two female officers on our ship walked out of the elevator and turned their heads, seeming to recognize him. My legs went limp. The women turned and headed straight toward me, and left with no other option, I jumped out of my armchair and lunged for the nearest door. Once outside I ran around the street and snuck back in through a side door. I found Easy by the elevators looking painfully exposed and pulled him into an elevator.

Six hours in the bathtub together, smoking cigarettes, drinking whiskey, we forged the sex of starvation, physical passion that permeated the room with the nicotine vapors.

Afterward we tried to wait for the safety of port visits, where we got better at finding hotels that no one frequented, but these visits were few. One was in Brunei, a country that would soon grant the death penalty to those like us. We didn't bother with a hotel there, but we did find our way to a restaurant bathroom. The danger and risk of that act would take years to comprehend.

Back on the frigate, we searched for locked spaces, dark corners. We tried the boatswain's locker at the very front of the ship, which had two watertight doors, each with eight dogs that had to be opened, one at a time. We were confident that no one could take us by surprise. But our first time in that sweaty space, half-clothed, we heard the sound of a door being unlocked. As each dog clicked open, our stomachs sunk.

"What will we say?" I whispered, squeezing his sweaty forearm.

"I don't know," he whispered back, looking this way and that. He pointed to the angle irons—shelflike support beams that reinforced the hull of the boat and doubled as storage space for all kinds of greasy lines and levers used for mooring the boat. "Climb into the gear locker."

I zipped up my coveralls and climbed the bulkhead as the first door opened. Easy pushed me upward as the second door began to click. We heard the first dog unlock, then the second. I climbed onto the shelf—feeling anchor-chain grease smear all over me—into the rigging and tackle, and pulled piles of heavy rope over me to hide. The loose fibers from the coarse rope stuck to my greased skin like feathers.

A third dog opened. Then silence. I held my breath, then a footstep, two. The intruder disappeared, closed the first door. We heard the sounds of dogs shutting. After an excruciating amount of time, I crawled out of the gear and slid out to the smoke deck while doing my best to shake off the fibers and wipe off the grease. A few minutes later, Easy joined me and we stared at the dark sea night, pretending that nothing at all could possibly connect us.

This became our routine—close calls and forbidden sex—although we made sure to find better spaces that didn't threaten us with getting caught. We would meet in the dark of night, relieve each other of the stresses and the silence that the job required, then make our way, one at a time, out to the smoke deck for a midnight cigarette. Eventually I became the sole technician on the ship's gun mount—a two-story cannon with a vaultlike space that was secured from the inside by a hulking watertight door. Like Easy's bosun's pipe, I carried the gun mount's many keys on a lanyard that hung at my hip and jangled as I walked about the ship. That wonderful MK 75 gun mount would become our private apartment for the rest of our deployment.

Each of the four walls of the gun mount housed shelves that contained missile canisters stacked in rows twenty high. The revolving magazine—which resembled an enormous cylinder from a six-shooter revolver—was suspended in the center of the space, free-hanging, and housed eighty of the blue-tipped ammunition rounds. It could empty these rounds in under a minute. Higher still, up into the second story, was the barrel housing, where the rounds were transferred and the firing commenced. Inside this vault of gunnery equipment, we made ourselves a home.

I'd set up a workingman's bookshelf from used ammo cans, in a pile that rose to the overhead. Inside the carefully arranged and lashed gunnery boxes were heaps of literature. I was deep into the transcendentalists: Emerson and Thoreau. Next to them was a copy of Whitman's *Leaves of Grass*, which my father had given me in high school. In Whitman I found camaraderie. A nurse during the Civil War, his poetry was considered scandalous by some; he could not be open about his sexuality. He wrote in *Drum Taps*: "As I lay my head in your lap camerado . . . I confess I have urged you onward with me, / and still urge you, without the least idea what is our destination, / Or whether we shall be victorious, or utterly quell'd or defeated." Like Whitman, I am compelled to serve, to stand by my brothers in arms, in wartime toward peace, but I too am considered scandalous, legally bound to hide my sexuality, my love. As he risked and urged onward, so do I, filled with the hope that love can flourish.

I can't say that Easy and I always abided by discretion. One night the two of us fell asleep atop a yoga mat on the deck together below the bookshelf. It was our only full night together that deployment. Like all the decks of the ship, it was made of nonskid material: hard and sharp to give traction to sailors walking in rough seas. But we'd found such comfort in each other that we slept well through that night, waking only to the sound of the reveille bells. Fear flooded the space as we both clamored to dress ourselves. Had we been seen? Easy quickly headed to the smoke deck, and I followed shortly thereafter.

A time or two, people did seem to notice that Easy and I would smoke at about the same time every night, but we always blew them off. We play video games together, we'd say, like a lot of other guys did at night on the ship. No one ever asked which ones. No one ever pointed out that I didn't even have a video game console in the gun mount.

Eventually I had had enough of hiding, and on my social media page I decided to change my orientation to gay. In so doing, I had transgressed the military's Don't Ask, Don't Tell policy. For that brief moment, I felt unanchored to other people's ideas about love. It felt expansive and oceanic and free.

There was a lot back then that was not asked and not told. Inside the lower level of the gun magazine were heaps of used ammunition canisters filled with trash. Once every few weeks, in the shadow of night, my supervisors took us to the gun mount and lined us up in a chain gang that extended down the hatchway ladder and out the starboard bulkhead door, each man within arm's reach of the next.

One time I was situated at the final watertight door, straddled between the steel frame of the ship and the opaque darkness of the ocean. We used pike tools to poke holes into metal ammunition canisters before throwing them overboard, where any splash they made was muffled by the noise of the waves. Oily rags, solvents, chemicals, perhaps even used paint canisters. The whitecapped waves were like teeth eager to consume.

Our supervisors called it night ops. We threw our waste overboard and watched as the canisters floated at first, then slowly filled and sank into the dark waters. A wreckage of trash trailed behind us like the flotsam from shipwrecks that survivors use to cling to the surface. I imagined them slowly sinking, never reaching the sea floor but instead piling on the underwater ridges of trash mountains from decades, perhaps centuries, of dumping, an unseen, underwater wasteland. Everything seemed so backward. Loving Easy was punishable by discharge, but throwing trash overboard was standard practice. I felt like the debris I threw out to the sea.

Night ops were a regular part of being on deployment, especially when a port visit was canceled and the ship began to overflow with trash. Our ship had a plastic waste compactor that turned the myriad plastic refuse into giant discs that were easily stowed away. But what of the rest? What of my legacy on the waters I traveled? Like the trash, I felt expendable, easily discarded, and began to see how our society floated on this concept of expendability. On the smoke deck, my hands stained with chemicals, I marred my lungs again and again with the markings of containment, hoping to forget. At some point Easy would appear, his greasy forearm resting on mine as he took the cigarette from my mouth, lit his with it, and gently put it back between my lips. He'd leave his arm next to mine as we leaned against the angle irons and looked beyond the ship that stayed us. In resignation, I threw my used cigarette butts to the sea.

In the final months of that first deployment, I was hit on by another sailor. Easy revealed to me that this man had molested him in his sleep. But he made me promise to never tell anyone. The sailor also threatened my life if I spoke about it. But once we returned to our home port of Everett, Washington, the JAG lawyers called me in for questioning and I told them everything I knew. They said they'd heard similar stories and would start an official investigation. The court-martial began, and with it came a series of inquiries into my illegal relationship with Easy. As gay men, we could not change our designation of dishonorable; we were the military's refuse. Our new classification—and my broken promise to Easy—pulled us apart.

I began my second deployment without him and the investigation still ongoing. The court-martial had not yet been scheduled, but its certainty constantly worried me. We sailed south toward Central America, the Pacific Ocean reflecting an incessant, scorching sun. I was often the only sailor at the top of the ship, surrounded on all sides by a blinding landscape of glimmering water and light. When I had first arrived, I enthusiastically climbed on top of the barrel of the gun mount and rode it like my grandfather rode broncos in Montana. Now the greatest effort I could command was leaning over the barrel as though over a fence that divided my life.

My future was in the hands of Commander Bradbury, a man I knew nothing about. Though the trial centered on Easy's abuser, my role as a witness was based on the credibility of my testimony, and this invited investigations into my character. It was now official that I broke the law of Don't Ask, Don't Tell. My commanding officer was required by law to discharge me, and the decision of how to go about doing so would be his alone. But when I was summoned to appear, it was not at the CO's quarters, where business was normally conducted, but at the office of the command master chief, the highest-ranking enlisted man on the boat. When I arrived at the door, which was adorned with the golden knot-work of boatswain mates, I knocked three times and stated my rank. I stepped into the room and saluted the CO with the usual decorum. Master chief shut the door behind me. The room shrunk to a point of vibrating suffocation.

"I think you know why you are here," the commanding officer said.

"Yes, sir. I do, sir."

"Then let's talk about this bluntly. As long as I've had command here, I've heard of your outstanding reputation. You've never been in any kind of trouble, and you've garnered the respect of the crew. So these recent developments have an obvious impact on the ship as a whole."

He seemed to walk a winding cliff over the course of his monologue, and I followed his every word, trying to decipher what his ultimate decision would be.

"This impasse is not beneficial to our cause," he went on. "I say this so that you understand the position you have placed us in."

Pinpricks of fear raced down my spine. My breath was stolen and thrust out of my lungs like an oceanic wind.

"With that said, we thought it appropriate to deal with this issue immediately and not drag it out through the deployment. In our eyes you have represented the Navy's core values with unswerving devotion. Even in the midst of hardship, you've upheld our core values of honor, courage, and commitment."

I could not speak. There was a smile in his eyes as his face maintained its stoic façade.

"That concludes our meeting, petty officer," master chief said, extending his arm toward the door.

We stood, and I saluted my CO. He looked me directly in the eye, and an expression that reminded me of my mother passed across his gaze, as if I were his own, of the same blood. I did an about-face and headed for the door, but then I heard his voice behind me: "One more thing, petty officer…"

I turned back around and saw a look of authority once again on his face.

"No more 'friends.'"

I locked the gun mount's door behind me and collapsed to the floor in the same place that I'd held Easy. Thoreau's words from *Civil Disobedience* came to me from my bookshelf as I lay alone on that nonskid: "Unjust laws exist; shall we be content to obey them, or shall we endeavor to amend them, and obey them until we have succeeded, or shall we transgress them at once." The shame of my idealism, my insistence on truth, was the reason for Easy's absence. It was the reason we were caught. But he was violated, not only by the accused; he was violated by a law that silenced his identity, his love, and even his rights as a victim. I could not abide the injustice. I had to act. Wreckage upon wreckage, I reached for a better world.

Later that night on the smoke deck, I held a cigarette in my left hand and kept the open pack in my quivering right, ready to light up the next in anxious succession. I'd survived that day, but a few weeks later I would be flown from Panama back to Everett for the court-martial. Suddenly, instead of relishing the smoke that filled my lungs, I began to choke. In the center of so many forces beyond my control, I realized that smoking was one of the few things I could control. In that moment I couldn't know that it would take me years to quit the habit, and so many more beyond that for my lungs to heal. Or that, like the scars on my lungs, oppression is written in the body, so deep that it can be passed through our DNA.

The ship surged through the black waters spreading great clouds of chartreuse light, marking our path with the tail of a comet. The bioluminescence offered me solace. In it, I realized my CO had offered me a chance to heal, if I could see the years through.

The cigarette burned to the filter, leaving a long branch of ash in its place. It singed my fingertips. I raised my hand to throw it overboard but stopped. I turned to the tin can I'd seldom used and tossed the butt onto the small pile of ash. Closing the open pack in my right hand, I lost myself to the marvel of the lights below.

Assaulted and Silenced

I think there were seven witnesses, but I remember only four distinct faces.

We were sitting in a waiting room of the judge advocate general's building of Naval Base Kitsap on Washington state's Kitsap Peninsula. Inside the courtroom there were high ceilings, brass fixtures, pews for spectators, flags, and wooden jury benches that rose up like stadium seating. Men in dress uniform stood as sentinels at every exit and by every important figure present.

But the waiting room for us witnesses was an unadorned office with a long meeting table. The room was tense. It was the kind of atmosphere that sent every occupant into some sort of physical reaction when someone inhaled too deeply: a cough, a repositioning of a chair, a quick lap around the long table. All the others were straight men, except for my ex-boyfriend. Every man in the room had been a victim of sexual assault except me.

We'd been in the waiting room for more than a week because the trial was restricted to a nine-to-five schedule. Sailors are issued only one pair of dress blues, our most formal uniform, and after a week of fearful waiting the smell was intense. We were told not to talk among ourselves about the trial, which was ongoing, down a hallway with marble floors. Randomly, a court emissary would come into the room, state a name, and escort that individual to the courtroom. The face that returned to the room was profoundly changed, but no one was allowed to say anything about what they experienced. We searched the lines of each other's faces, trying to communicate without speech, trying to assuage the trepidation, the shame.

I'm reading Leo Tolstoy's *War and Peace*. The year is 2007. In the midst of all this drama, the book is giving me perspective, taking me elsewhere, making me feel less defined by the hapless narrative of this trial and part of the bigger tides of history.

My ex, Easy, breaks the monotonous silence.

"I wish I would have brought a book myself," he says. "I can't imagine I'll ever read one that big, though."

I drop the massive book onto the table with a loud thud. We laugh. There, for a moment, is the face of the man I fell for—gregarious, electric, alive. Too soon, it's gone.

"You're going to write something really important one day, Lance." Easy's words produce thunderheads in my chest. "Will you write something about me?"

"I'll try," I say, barely holding back the emotion.

I find it almost ironic that he is asking me to become a witness again, sometime in the future, by writing about him, about this. He didn't want me to speak up in the first place.

We were in Malaysia when he told me about the assault, told me never to tell. But I was young and idealistic, and I could not be silent. I confronted the accused. His only words were "I'm sorry." I took that as an admission of guilt, and when he later threatened my life if I told anyone, I was confident in the assumption that he was guilty.

For five months after that I didn't say anything. I asked Easy why he didn't want to come forward. He said he was ashamed that it had happened to him. It made him feel weak. He didn't want anyone on our ship to know about it. I understood, and

I dutifully held that secret. But months later, when our ship sailed back to the Pacific Northwest, I was called to the Naval Criminal Investigative Service (NCIS) and questioned about my interaction with the accused. Caught off guard and relieved to offload this growing secret, I told them everything that had happened. The kind NCIS agent assured me that I was doing the right thing.

Turns out there were other guys on the ship who had come forward with similar stories. It seemed the accused had a pattern. The agent said she couldn't tell me details, but what had happened to Easy had happened to others.

The accused had a leadership position as the petty officer in charge of the galley, where oncoming sailors had to work for two months when they first got aboard. Often, he made quick friends with the young sailors. This friendship turned into nights out drinking. For Easy, and for the others, a drunken night out would end with the young men passed out. And then later, according to their accounts, they would reportedly wake up in the middle of the night with the accused performing sexual acts on them against their will.

The NCIS agent told me that my account was a pivotal piece of the prosecution, that the death threats were an admission of guilt. But to me, my involvement didn't seem substantial, and it was predicated on a promise I made to Easy, which I broke.

That makes sitting in the waiting room all the more excruciating. I sit in a cloud of doubt. I know so little about this trial and yet am stuck in the middle of it.

It's my turn to testify. The shame. The uncertainty.

I'm escorted into the regal courtroom, with a full cast of the highest brass in the U.S. Navy. The sheer sight of all the ribbons and insignia puts me into a cave in my own mind. I want to hide, to be anywhere else other than here, to go back in time and not have said anything to anyone.

The prosecuting attorney goes over my testimony quickly. For the first time in my military career, I get the opportunity to speak out publicly.

Then the defense attorney begins his cross-examination. To my disbelief, he doesn't go after my meager involvement in the case. He doesn't try to dissuade the jury that the defendant made threats against my life. He doesn't even go into the hearsay quality of what I know about my ex-boyfriend's victimhood.

His voice is calm and direct. "What is your relationship with the other witness in your testimony?" he asks.

"He's my ex-boyfriend."

"Was this relationship active during your enlistment in the United States Navy?"

"Yes."

"So, you openly admit that you are in breach of the policy of Don't Ask, Don't Tell?"

"What do you mean?"

"Are you aware that you are breaking the law?"

The faces of the jury sharpen into focus. I had vaguely feared I would be kicked out for my testimony because of Don't Ask, Don't Tell, but there were more important issues related to the accused at hand, like sexual assault. It hadn't occurred to me that Don't Ask, Don't Tell would become the central focus of my testimony.

Sitting there on the witness stand, I am frozen. The defense attorney raises his voice to grab my attention, to force my words.

"Are you aware that you are breaking the long-standing military policy of Don't Ask, Don't Tell?"

The faces of the jury are like floodlights on me. I'm sweating profusely. As the accused's defense attorney highlights all the ways I am depraved and out of line and not to be trusted, as he stokes hatred of gay people into fiery expressions on the faces of the jury, I realize that Easy was right. I never should have spoken up. My witnessing is a failure here. Not only is the story I thought I was coming here to tell not being heard, but I am being attacked for something I cannot change about myself.

I stare at the faces of the jury, as if trying to memorize them, because I sense that they contain something, a secret, a truth that I will need later as I try to make sense of this whole debacle. They look like a mob of vengeful faces—except for one. I come across one kind expression. It is as if he is filled with shame over what he is here to do, what he is now a part of. He's unable to offer anything other than this apologetic look, but at least it's something.

"I repeat the question, for the third time, are you—"

After all of my insistence on telling the truth about what happened to Easy, it never occurs to me to lie.

"Yes," I say.

Back to the waiting room.

The next day Easy disappears into the courtroom to give his testimony. I try to lie with my facial expression, to encourage him and send some positivity his way. We're not allowed to talk about my testimony, but now I know what he is up against. And for him the courtroom will be so much worse.

After he leaves, I sit there filling up with anger—an anger that will take years to diminish. My inability to cope eventually leads, years later, to seeing a therapist. In therapy, I find out that victims of sexual assault are known to experience symptoms of PTSD throughout their lives. The therapist tells me about how much more likely LGBTQ people are to have substance abuse issues and become homeless, precisely because of unfair systems and policies like Don't Ask, Don't Tell. The shame that I feel at that moment in the waiting room—shame for adding to the weight of my ex's struggle—grows for years, into a gnarled and invasive vine that extends through so many areas of my life. I'll find out years later that so many of these negative outcomes will tarnish Easy's future.

When Easy comes back into the waiting room, he looks physically changed, unfamiliar. He was the last witness. Though the tension of the room is gone, it's muggy, and we sit in a swamp of resignation.

The verdict. All the witnesses, the men who've been assaulted, are allowed to go into the courtroom for the reading, but only my ex and I elect to go. I sit next to him. This is the closest we've been physically since his great breakdown and our subsequent breakup.

The accused is acquitted on all but the smallest of charges. If the emotional haze of memory serves me right, he was found guilty of fraternization—when a superior has unprofessional involvement with subordinates. A charge like that was considered so minor that it was normally handled in-house and would never, on its own, make it all the way to a court-martial. As punishment, the accused must retire a few months sooner than planned, with full benefits.

I'm not sure I'll ever forgive myself for subjecting my ex to that terror. In the visceral pain of my own experience there was no comparison to the injuries he suffered, both in the initial assault and in the experience of that trial.

I wrote a novel to try to atone for my sin of bearing witness, to attempt to make something beautiful from the ashes—a novel about the downside of telling the truth. It's titled *Second-Class Sailors*. It sits, obscure. Easy read it, though, and he sent me a kind email thanking me for the telling.

In it, I gave him the name Danny. I had been trying to tell his story for more than a decade. I had been afraid to tell it, afraid of the repercussions, of what I'd lose from the telling. So much has been lost already. Would the telling affect my career? Would it affect Easy's career even more than the trial did? Would the accused really try to kill me? All this fear, and I wasn't even the one who was assaulted.

After the conclusion of the trial, we made our separate ways back to the mainland. He was headed to Everett, to finish out his enlistment at a shore-duty station. I was headed to Seattle, then back to the ship in Panama to finish my final deployment.

The one lucky thing that happened to us is that we were each able to finish our enlistments and voluntarily leave with honorable discharges before someone had time to dishonorably discharge us with Don't Ask, Don't Tell. We could have reenlisted, but the policy could have been used against us at any moment because of our testimonies. As my therapist said, "Sounds like eviction to me."

As Easy and I waited in line for the ferry, we grabbed coffee. Most of these moments were spent in silence, our mode. The ferry bells called us back to our cars, and I lunged for the chance to say something of worth.

"No amount of apology could ever..."

"You did"—his voice cracked as he attempted to control it—"the right thing."

My eyes welled up. We turned to make our way back to our separate cars.

"Lance?" The word came out like a question, and I turned back toward him. He was maybe fifteen feet away. "Thank you."

In the belly of the ferry, the windows of my car steamed up from the added humidity.

I haven't seen him since.

Discharge

I walk down the haze-gray passageway of the frigate USS *Rodney M. Davis,* clad in coveralls perfumed with the stark smell of gunpowder and the saccharine odors of gun lubricant. Down the hatchway, through white-painted angle irons, past the cramped mess-deck tables where the crew hurriedly eats meals, and across the blue-and-white-speckled linoleum, I find the coffee dispenser and fill my mug with the thick, stale liquid. On my way back up above decks, I walk by a black-and-white portrait of the ship's namesake, Rodney M. Davis, uniformed in his Marine regalia: white cap with black rim and a gold Marine emblem pinned to the center, black coat with gold buttons down the front, and piping across his chest and left shoulder. His rank is stitched to the fabric of his right arm. The photo is candid. A partial framed picture is behind his right shoulder, and it looks as if he's standing in a doorway. The look on his face, is it amused? Is that a smile trying to break out of his military bearing? He seems like a guy I'd want to hang out with. If things were different.

If you look up what happened to Sergeant Davis, you won't find much. Official reports detail a heroic man who served in the Vietnam War and was posthumously awarded the Medal of Honor for his courageous last act. He exemplified the core values of the military in the discharge of his duties: Honor, Courage, and Commitment. As I walk across the steel embodiment of his heroism, I wonder what his life was like.

When I make it to my destination, I use the lanyard slung around my left shoulder to unlock the vault door of the MK 75 gun magazine and close the hulking watertight door behind. Sweet reprieve. I inhale deeply, knowing it will be the last communion with this dear old friend, this grand cannon. Now, at twenty-two, I have almost completed my four-year enlistment. It's a funny thing to feel a kinship with an inanimate object, much less a weapon of war, but we've sailed the seas together, and in many respects it has been my closest confidant throughout the duration.

With my head held low, I walk through the gun magazine and touch the three-foot-high ammunition rounds, cold metal, smooth, sleek. With Sergeant Davis on my mind, I ponder the complexities of his experience. He grew up in Macon, Georgia, during segregation. As an African American, he served his country while racial riots were erupting around the country. Jim Crow laws were still being enforced in his hometown. What did he think of his place in all that turmoil? He was a Black man in charge of white men during a time when that was dangerous. Did that understanding give him pause in any way?

I imagine him in the trenches in Vietnam. Explosions a constant threat from the enemy seeking to kill him and his men. Gunfire slicing through the air, an ever-present reminder of death on the edge of every moment. He thinks of his daughters, his wife. Will he ever see them again? Their innocence, so many worlds away from this violence. His camouflage is filthy from all this time in the dirt and dank latrines they live near. His feet throb from sores, and the chafing from his soiled clothes cuts lacerations into his skin. Death is only staved off by the gun in his hands and the guns in the hands of his men. Everything is happening so fast. Then he notices a rock tumbling through the air as it lands on the wet, earthen floor of the trench. The rock is not a rock. It's a grenade. In this moment he doesn't look at the faces around him, these faces that are a different color than his, even though it's hard to tell under all the grime that covers them. He doesn't stop to think about what to do and if it's worth it. He doesn't turn to run. His dark eyes steel over with the power of his reaction. Diving toward the grenade, he grabs it, cold metal in his muddy hands, and pulls it to his loins, covering it with all the flesh he has, curling his body in a ball of determination, of protection, until he is no longer a body. The remnants of his love cover every surface of the trench. His men are alive and continue to fight.

If he ever thought about his difference, he didn't act on it. All the men in the trench with him were white.

As an openly gay man placed in a supervisory role on this ship during the Don't Ask, Don't Tell era, I can't help but ponder how he managed these issues. How can a gay man be in charge of teaching the crew of straight men how to shoot, be in charge of the ship's largest artillery, and still be at the mercy of a law designed to end his career if he is made known? How can a Black man serve his country and die for it, be granted the Medal of Honor, and not be allowed, by law, to be buried in his hometown? He was buried where all the Black people were buried, outside the city limits. The bravery of Sergeant Davis is so much greater when viewed in the context of his life and his time.

Under the gun, I climb through to the interior where all the hydraulic and pneumatic machinery is housed. Higher still, I climb up to the second story, to the barrel housing, where the rounds are transferred into the barrel assembly and the firing commences. The smells are intoxicating, conjuring visceral memories: the jolting thunder of the gun firing eighty shots in quick succession. My body braces. The smells evoke power.

Hidden next to the breechblock of the barrel is a dented soda can with the acrid smell of wet and burnt tobacco. It is my source of defiance during this strict enlistment, a way for me to counter the angst in my bones over what I've been through. I pull out a Parliament Light and inhale the flame from my lighter. To get caught smoking in here would elicit a heavy penalty, but I do it anyway. It's worth the risk while the smoke deck is closed—mostly during refueling or drug-interdiction operations when we search fishing vessels for smuggled goods—but tonight is different, tonight is the final one, and this sweet communion has to be revisited one last time. But this punishment would be fitting for the crime—unlike others. Inhaling the vapors, I fondle the slick surface of the lubricated metal. A few clicks of levers here, a few turns of gears there: a somber symphony, saturated by the clouds of nicotine. I lean back against the rocking arms that bring the ammunition from vertical to horizontal: a mechanical embrace, soothing arms that held me while out to sea.

The journey to this moment wasn't planned. I had no intention of being a sailor on a warship. When I enlisted, I had a very different vision of where I would end up. Yet somehow, I ended up here. Ended up a witness in a criminal trial over the sexual assault of multiple men on this ship, both gay and straight. That would be the cotter pin of my experience here, the defining piece in the machine that kept it all together but also threatened to make it all fall apart. It placed me at odds with a law that imperiled my continued existence in the military. By speaking out and bearing witness, I exposed my life to the inquiry of investigators and officially outed myself. Yet I did have a choice in it all. Abiding by the censorship of my identity was tolerable for a time. It was the way my generation had been raised and indoctrinated. But I was already fed up with that silence, and when it came to censoring the rights of victims to tell the truth, or betraying the men I served with and what happened to them, it became a line I could not help but cross. I had to speak out, to fight the compounding injustices. Sergeant Davis didn't seem to have a breaking point in his story. I did. What would he have done in my situation?

The night before I left for boot camp, I sat in a hotel room alone, and it started to hit me: I was leaving everything behind. It was unclear when, or if, I'd see my mother, my father, my siblings again. The friendships I'd grown over the years would never be the same. I had signed a multiyear contract relinquishing control of my life to the government, and there was no going back.

They flew me to Chicago, where a group of recruits and I were loaded into a bus and dropped off at the entrance of the military base at Great Lakes. The screaming began instantaneously. Our only option was to absorb it without response. They took our clothes. They buzzed our heads. They herded us around like cattle and trained us to be obedient. We acquiesced. We were there by choice and were ready to serve.

Great pride sat lightly on our newfound correct posture. Military bearing became us. We ironed our underwear into tight little envelopes of starched precision. We snapped quickly to attention. I succeeded at physical and organizational drills and was promoted.

We had been primed for silence, trained efficiently. The chief in charge of my battalion used to stand at the entrance to the large open shower rooms and watch us. He was in power. We were nothing and had no one to complain to.

There were murmurs of him doing more than just watching. He began to pick his favorites. One evening during the period when we were required to organize our lockers, the chief called me into his office. It was situated at the front of the large barracks room, with a window that allowed him to look out and watch us. Through that window, he could see everything that we did.

He directed me to sit under the window, on the floor, positioning me so that no one outside could see me. Once I was in the spot, he handed me a cookie and told me to eat it. I didn't know what to make of this request, but I did what I was told. He watched me as he sat in a chair, a strange expression on his face. He leaned back, his eyes gazing downward at me. When I was released back to the ranks, the guys were concerned, asking me what had happened in there. I told them I had eaten a cookie, but their concern didn't abate. He continued to call me into his office in the evenings, always a cookie on hand. They had no taste, and I worked hard to swallow the paste that caked in my dry mouth. I had a flimsy reason to interact with him, as I had been promoted to dental yeoman—the individual responsible for scheduling appointments and keeping detailed records—but every time he called me into the office a deep rage filled me, one that I couldn't allow to be visible on the surface.

Then some middle-management petty officers caught him doing something overtly wrong—leering at a lone man in the shower—and they reported him. He was relieved of his position as our lead but kept his rank and was put in charge of another unit. Our petty officers apologized to us and said that his conduct did not fit with our core values. Still, not one of us had a voice in that scenario. Even as the issue got rectified, we were kept silent.

It was only later that I realized what it looked like from the outside of the chief's office as he sat in front of his desk and I ate his cookie on the floor. All you would have been able to see through the window was him leaning back in his chair, a strange expression on his face, his arms lifted to cradle his head in his hands, his eyes looking downward.

After boot camp, I began Gunner's Mate A school on the other side of the Great Lakes Base. It was in a large, green-tinted, glass building that housed huge cannons inside the gleaming structure, an emerald in the otherwise uniformly redbrick compound. Whenever we were on the sidewalks with our gunnery class, we marched as one unit around the masonry buildings that resembled a college campus. Stepping to the cadence, our class leader screamed, "Gun school, what do we do?"

The entirety of our squadron would respond in a full-throated bellow, "Kill!"

On each step he would counter, "What?"

"Kill!"

"What?"

Each step was a beat to the counter and repeat.

After gunnery school, I was sent to join the Dive Motivators: SEALS, whose job it was to prepare us for our upcoming BUD/S training during the summer. They called us Scruffs. I was a strong candidate for the endurance portion of the training. After finding my stride and becoming one of the three fastest runners in the group, I solidified my place by becoming the fastest swimmer, beating out a lead candidate who had been there for months and had held the title his whole tenure. It was a proud moment and helped me handle being one of the weakest at pull-ups and only marginal at push-ups.

One day during training, the instructors told us they had a new game. They pulled out an Oscar Mayer wiener whistle that hung on a lanyard around one of their necks and was about an inch long. The game was simple: whoever fell from the pull-up bar first lost and had to wear the wiener whistle around their neck for the rest of the day. We got into position at the bars that surrounded the Olympic-size pool, and at the sound of the whistle jumped to grab the bars. I didn't get a good grip and fell immediately.

As the first wiener, I had to whistle wherever I went that day. With such a dubious title, I looked for ways to overcome my luck. Another common form of punishment for falling short of our drills was to be forced to walk on all fours with our asses in the air—a moving form of the yoga position downward-facing dog. Whenever anyone was forced to walk on all fours that day, I'd join them in the punishment, whistling my wiener and taking the attention off of my fellow recruit. It made the punishment for both of us fun, and I was glad for it.

I wasn't the wiener the next day or any day after that. But I had made an impression on the instructors. Later I would find out that after every batch of Scruffs was sent away to BUD/S training, the instructors placed bets on the few they thought would make it. Of the handful of men they chose from our class, a bet was placed on me.

After months of constant training, we were sent to Coronado, California, and the real training was set to begin. With nine months in the Navy and still a teenager, I found myself at one of the most prestigious military schools in the world. We began Indoctrination Phase, the first of four phases of training, and I was performing well. Days were filled with physical drills, along with pep talks about why we were there and if we were wholly dedicated to becoming warriors. They made it clear that even our families would play second fiddle to our jobs. Most of us would end up divorced and rarely seeing our kids if we continued down this road. Were we okay with that? More importantly, could we kill? They told us there was no shame in walking away. Some people weren't cut out to be weapons of war. What I found most surprising was the openness of the SEAL instructors, their humility, and how they treated us as something close to equals. It felt like we were all on the same team.

The smoke from inside the gun mount has gotten dense, so I turn the wheel of the hatchway door just enough to let some of the smoke out. The butt of the smoked cigarette drops into the soda can with a fizzle.

When I left Coronado, I went through a crisis. drowning in the uncertainty of the religion of my youth, my concept of God, my political affiliation, my family life, my understanding of who I was as a person. I was a man overboard, a man without a ship, and I could not swim. There was nothing to grasp ahold of to help me float. I could not breathe. A great sea change began as I sank. The upheaval of this tempest, and the aftermath of its destruction, took me to depths I had never known. I was alone, and all I had was an unflattering understanding of who I was. Words filled my lungs like water. *Faggot. Failure. Abomination.*

Obscurely, like light from the great height of that very distant surface, the first rays of understanding came to me—of how to love, and to love myself. In that alien landscape, that lonely and vast seabed, I decided to swim that great distance toward the surface. Out of the abyss.

I promised myself that I would find a way to live openly. I would not hide anymore. Although this ship was not in my plan, it's taught me about the cost of living authentically, the cost of truth. I've gained a sort of satisfaction from having conviction, of standing for something. Of standing for others. I have finally found a voice to speak with. But even after all this time, I have still not found a home. This is my last option to finish what I started. I could still reenlist and get an assignment back to BUD/S. I could go back and become a SEAL, like our class leader had done on his second attempt. Most people take two or three tries to graduate. The sands of the Silver Strand were still waiting for me. I've kept myself in the same physical condition, except for the cigarettes, but I can quit smoking. My experience on this ship has given me perspective. I'm stronger than the teenager I was when I first arrived at BUD/S. Should I go back? Are they ready for me? Am I ready to break that barrier and become the first openly gay Navy SEAL?

Not after what happened here. Not after barely surviving this trial as a witness. I'm lucky to get out with an honorable discharge. All the effort to become a Navy SEAL would be wasted. Don't Ask, Don't Tell still exists, and I'm a documented homosexual. If I stay in, a dishonorable discharge is inevitable.

Rodney M. Davis, what a strange coincidence to serve aboard your namesake, to see your example of fighting for what's right even if your country doesn't allow you the full rights of a citizen. Your example empowers me to continue onward. I've been given that opportunity. I'm still alive, and I have no great injury, except perhaps the amputation of this career. If you could pay the ultimate sacrifice, then I can take these limitations imposed upon me, hold fast to a hope for the future, and help build a better world, as you have done.

The phone rings in the small room in the magazine below. I climb back down through the gun to the gun mount captain's control room and grab the phone that hangs above the control panel. The messenger tells me to go to the command master chief's office. Shit, did someone rat on me for smoking in the gun?

I make my way out of the magazine, through a short vestibule and around a corner, and arrive at the open door of the master chief's office. I knock three times, stand at attention, and state my name, Gunner's Mate Second Class Garland.

"GM2, come into my office," Master Chief James declares in short coughs of syllables.

I come to ease from the position of attention, walk into the confined quarters as he nods for me to sit in the small leather chair situated in front of his ornate desk. Knot-work emboldened with golden paint covers every frame, corner, and edge of the office. A proud boatswain's mate, he undoubtedly fashioned all the lines himself.

"GM2, I'm going to convince you to abandon this god-awful idea of yours to get out of the Navy." This is just a setup. His cadence is only vaguely picking up steam.

"Well, sir, I've always wanted to go to college, and now I finally get the cha—"

"That's all well and good, my boy, but I'm about to offer you something that no man in his right mind could turn down: the chance to be one of three instructors of the illustrious three-inch gunnery school. Your gun. Only three men every four years get this opportunity, and I've pulled the strings to make it happen."

Breath escapes me for a moment. My gun. I had not seen this coming. Master chief sees my hesitation and strikes again.

"Moreover, since it is shore duty, you will have plenty of time to complete a degree, after work hours. You'll have a regular nine-to-five for the next few years."

The information settles over me like gunpowder silt. A fine opportunity, but it is not aligned with reality. After what happened, I'd be doomed to a dishonorable. No money for college after that. No benefits. Nothing.

"Will the new command get my file?"

The immediacy of his advance slows. He pulls at his left ear. "You will also get an early advancement to petty officer first class, and with your track record you will be a chief before your next reenlistment."

I don't move. My lips don't hesitate their hard line. The question is the end of the road.

"Do you hear me, GM2? You will be a chief before you're thirty. Your whole career, life, will be made. You will have freedom like few others dream of. You can retire before you're forty."

The room, empty now, is as vast as the vacant sea. I had been thrown into a position of authority with that gun mount. At one point I was the only gunner onboard. During a few major casualties to the gun system, I scoured the manuals of the electronic, pneumatic, and hydraulic systems in order to find the faults, and I'd been awarded multiple Navy achievement medals for my ability to rectify the issues. One casualty had been during high-profile war games with multiple other navies when a misfire happened at the height of training. I had to clear the misfired round without killing anyone and get the systems back online to continue training. I managed to do that, and from that point on I was invited into the officers' quarters for all debriefings and prefire meetings with the commanding officer. I don't remember there being any other enlisted personnel below the rank of chief in those closed-door meetings.

"I am deeply moved, master chief, but I have to ask again. Will the new command know about my sexuality?"

He leans back into his chair. "What do you mean?"

"My file, the trial. Will the new command get it? Will my new CO get the information?"

"Yes, he will," he says, and raises his hand as in the form of a salute, but instead he covers his right eye and presses his fingers roughly into his eyebrow.

I think of the reason I've reached this impasse. Truth. Was it worth it?

"I appreciate this incredible offer. It is an honor, sir, and I wish I could take it, but I think I'll stick with my plan to go to college."

"You joined the Navy while still in high school, didn't you? Well, let me tell you, it's not easy out there. You have no idea what you're about to get into."

"No one in my family has ever been to a university. If I get out now, I'll get to." Leaving all this opportunity on the table because of an unjust law feels like I'm receiving an honorable eviction. The choice doesn't feel like mine. It feels like it's been written for me.

My response is clearly not what he'd expected. "This law won't last forever, GM2, and if you had any sense in that bull head of yours you'd see the future ahead of you." He continues to fume, stands, rounds his desk, and ushers me quickly out of his office.

He was right. On September 20, 2011, four years into the future and a whole enlistment cycle away, Don't Ask, Don't Tell would be repealed.

But in this moment, I see no future here. The slamming door mutes his rant. I stand in the vacant passageway for some time, staring at the brazen knot-work on his closed door. There's nothing left to do but make my way back to my packing.

Out of Desolation

On leave after a six-month deployment across the Pacific Ocean, I made my way with a pair of friends to a mythic locale we'd only seen in our mind's eye, through the writings of Jack Kerouac.

Streamers of froth trailed behind us as our water taxi marred the smooth face of the lake. A steady rumble of the boat's engine was the only sound in the secluded backcountry of Ross Lake, past the noise of Highway 20, into the rugged wonderland of the North Cascades.

Kerouac's words seemed to whisper with the engine's hoarse voice. "There was nowhere to go but everywhere, so just keep rolling under the stars."

Raindrops fell as the boat pulled up to a seasonal dock at a campsite called Lightning Creek. We disembarked with our loads of gear as the boat operator gruffly stated, "I'll be back to pick you up at noon in two days." Without further ceremony he was gone, and with him the only other manmade sounds.

We set up camp and made small talk to stave off the silence.

I had camped before, as a kid with my family. But at the age of twenty-two, this was my first excursion into the backcountry: twelve miles away from the nearest road, no cell service. No way to contact someone if something went wrong.

∞

More than half a century before my own pilgrimage, a not-yet-famous Jack Kerouac also followed a writer he admired into the woods. The year was 1955, and he and Gary Snyder shared a cabin outside of Berkeley.

An outdoorsman versed in Buddhist poetics, Snyder had found enlightenment as a fire lookout in the North Cascades and encouraged Kerouac to apply for a post. Kerouac, a city boy, was eager to experience the spiritualism of the backcountry but possessed no survival skills to rely on in the wild.

The men set their sights on Matterhorn Peak in Yosemite National Park as training grounds. On the trail, ebullient with enthusiasm, Snyder stripped off his clothes. Kerouac watched his muse's bare butt frolic up the ridges, deeply envious of his lightheartedness. At base camp that night, the men reeled with the intellectual agility of their ideas.

The next day, the air thinned as they ascended the 12,280-foot peak, and Kerouac's exuberance turned to dread. He was out of his element. Snyder coached him up the mountain: "The secret of this kind of climbing is like Zen. Don't think. Just dance along."

Nearing the craggy summit of Matterhorn, Kerouac lost his motivation and did not make it to the top. For the rest of the hike, he turned sullen and argumentative with Snyder, who had easily crested the mountaintop.

The encounter foreshadowed Kerouac's tumultuous relationship with the wilderness—and his psyche. Both struggles came to a head for him the next summer as a lone fire lookout atop Desolation Peak.

A few months before our camping adventure, in my last year of enlistment, we three sailors had voyaged across the Pacific Ocean aboard our Navy frigate. We took turns standing watch on the uppermost deck of the ship, at twin .50 caliber machine guns, where we monitored the watery wilderness for any other maritime vessels. Jason, a libertarian from San Francisco, lent me his copy of *Desolation Angels*, which chronicles Kerouac's summer on Desolation Peak. The book grasped hold of my imagination, and soon I had read much of Kerouac's body of work.

The ship's watch deck became my own desolation lookout, a place for me to sift through the mire of my life and struggles to accept my identity.

Through sixty-three lonely nights as the fire lookout on Desolation, Kerouac awoke to clamoring wind and often to the imposing figure of Hozomeen Mountain looming through the windows. "At night at my desk in the shack I see the reflection of myself in the black window. . . . Courage it takes to live and face all this iron impasse."

Through his prose, I found a catharsis as well as a vocabulary to describe the depths of my own plight as I stood guard over an empty sea. Kerouac's descriptions of desperation, shame, loneliness, and self-loathing were everything that I felt about my own experience. His tone and his infatuation with other men reminded me of myself. I saw a deep connection between how he felt about the men in his life and my own attractions to men while being in the closet. I would learn that Kerouac's sexuality became a threat to his survival while he was in college, where the difference between being a witness of self-defense or being an accomplice to murder was entirely contingent on whether he was gay. Kerouac's fellow student at Columbia, Lucian Carr, had murdered a man who was also his lover and ran to Kerouac for help. When he was arrested for murder, he claimed to the police that he acted in self-defense. The police arrested Kerouac as a material witness, and in his fictional autobiography, *The Vanity of Duluoz: An Adventurous Education, 1935–46*, he writes a scene where the police's interrogation chiefly came down to the question: What would you do if a queer grabbed your cock? There is so much that can't be known about this situation, but from my experience, I see this as a choice for young Kerouac: to be gay was to be an accomplice to murder, to be straight was to survive. What kind of choice is that?

I could relate to this penalty for being gay and how much it could cost someone even if it didn't pertain to the actual case at hand. Because I stood up as a witness against sexual assault, my experience of the trial became more about my sexuality than about the allegations against a man accused of sexual assault. The threat of getting kicked out under Don't Ask, Don't Tell made clear to me the cost of loving men. In Kerouac I saw a vision of myself in a time not entirely unlike the one I inhabited, and I felt like we understood each other. As I stood watch from my own lookout in the Pacific Ocean, I felt like I saw through Kerouac's eyes.

He was right when he wrote, "The sound of silence is all the instruction you'll ever get."

At Lightning Creek, my friends and I awoke to puddles of water in our six-person tent. After a hearty breakfast of bacon cooked by campfire and black coffee laced with Irish whiskey, we made our soggy way to the trailhead and began our ascent. The hike was steep, up 4,400 feet of elevation over 6.8 miles of waterlogged pine forest. Sweat fell in droplets down the ravine of my spine.

Jason separated himself from the group. I worked hard to keep up as our third friend, Patrick, fell far behind. Soon I was alone in the forest, wondering if Kerouac knew what it felt like to be alone and in the closet.

Fellow writer Gore Vidal says he did. In 1953 a night of drinking together in Manhattan's Greenwich Village took a turn on a street corner, with Kerouac swinging his body around a light pole like a stripper. In Vidal's memoir—published after Kerouac's death—he claims the encounter turned amorous. In his novel *The Subterraneans*, Kerouac sets a vague scene: "[Vidal] is a well-known and perfectly obvious homosexual of the first water, my roaring brain—we go to his suite in some hotel—I wake up in the morning on the couch, filled with the horrible recognition, 'I didn't go back to Mardou's at all.'" Vidal's account is much more sexually explicit.

I knew a few men in the Navy who had one-night stands with other men and then hated themselves for it—and turned to blatant homophobia in the interest of reinstating their heterosexuality. In Kerouac I saw traces of the same story. Although he was married to three different women, I couldn't help but see correlations between my experience in the closet and his.

Despite his legendary freedom and his involvement with the queer characters of the Beat Generation, Kerouac's public life looked much like that of a suppressed 1950s straight male. Unlike his mentor Snyder, Kerouac did not find peace on the peak, and his affinity for the outdoors had dried up by the end of his lookout post. "Desolation adventure finds me finding at the bottom of myself abysmal nothingness worse than no illusion even my mind's in rags—"

For all of Kerouac's attempts to write his story, something more must have been hidden beneath it, something that drove him to drink himself down the river Styx.

Still alone on the trail, out of the trees I entered cinematic fields of subalpine meadows along Starvation Ridge. The uncannily named Jack Mountain and Nohokomeen Glacier emerged to the south. A serpentine Ross Lake meandered southward far below, the swells on its surface like scales the color of pewter. The dew-laden wildflowers of Indian paintbrush and lupine hung heavy on the stem. Rust- and violet-speckled hills of green grasses swayed in the light morning wind.

I was sweating thick and working out some of my angst. Kerouac, it occurred to me, navigated an age not entirely unlike my own. In the unedited scroll of *On the Road*, published for the first time in August 2007, Kerouac describes the homosexual exploits between his best friend, Neal Cassady, and Beat poet Allen Ginsberg, and used their real names instead of fictionalized names—Dean Moriarty and Carlo Marx—in the originally published version. Publishers censored this homosexual content, and Kerouac self-censored subsequent drafts in order to get his book published. If he couldn't even write honestly about his friends, how much harder would it have been to express his own truth?

I knew how it felt to be silenced. My childhood was controlled, to the point that I had almost no understanding of what it meant to be gay. The military, in turn, took up the charge of molding me into their version of who I should be.

I caught up with Jason, and we headed northward along a sparse ridgeline until, at last, the Buddhist-like hut of the fire lookout came into view. I stepped inside the humble structure and gazed out through the windows. The craggy, M-shaped Hozomeen peak loomed directly to the north, and a sea of mountain ranges spread out on all sides. A surreal moment transported me back to my post on the O2 level aboard my Navy frigate. Two chronologies merged into one.

As I stood in Kerouac's footprints, a new vision emerged on the horizon. I would climb peaks and rise above my inner demons. I would fight fire for a living instead of look for it as a spectator. I would find my own Dean Moriarty and love him openly. Kerouac's words came to mind once more: "Live, travel, adventure, bless, and don't be sorry." I looked out to the wilderness and added another word to his mantra. Love, and don't be sorry.

Recession

With an honorable discharge from the Navy, I was lucky. After completing my enlistment, I had a lot of different goals. Most of all, I wanted to be free to be myself and do what I wanted. I grew a beard, learning the art of maintaining it and how to keep it tamed. Next came enrollment in North Seattle College, a rented house a few blocks away with my Navy friend Tate, and the start of writing my Navy story. After a few classes in college, I discovered my strengths and my weaknesses. I failed a math class but got good grades in English and drama, receiving accolades for my portrayal of Brick in *Cat on a Hot Tin Roof*, a role and a mindset I was intimately acquainted with. I clashed with some of the teachers, thinking I was above the condescending, parentlike role they played with their teenage students. As the oldest person in most of my classes, with kids who were still in high school, I had a hard time adjusting and knowing where to fit. This didn't help my sense of identity. My thought process had been that getting out of the Navy would solve all my problems, but now I was faced with a world that didn't seem to care much if I succeeded, much less who I was. The camaraderie was lost, and I was as well.

Anger grew within me for the first time. A great root of darkness swelled from the seed of Don't Ask, Don't Tell. I began to drink daily, sitting on the porch of my rented house, where Tate and I would drink whiskey for hours, talking about life and philosophy. I named the concrete porch the Philosopher's Plateau, and we smoked cigarette after cigarette, chasing thought after thought, until I stumbled to my cot upstairs.

My family continued to fall apart, and my presence made no difference. My father fell into a darkness that bound him with a methadone addiction, among other drugs. His dark orbit pulled my youngest brother into the addiction with him, and soon the two were dangerous to be around. Theft, verbal abuse, crime—our family became a horror story, and the poison touched everything. I had to do something to stop the destruction. At a diner for our last meal together, I told my father there would always be a place for him if he could find his way back, but I could not follow him into the wasteland he had created with his life and with my little brother's. He was unrecognizable that day and didn't seem to care. He was already gone, and there was nothing I could do to help him or my baby brother. It felt worse than a family member dying, because it was living death. Now I see them like specters, am haunted by their ghostly figures that appear unexpectedly in random moments of my life.

I wrote voraciously, needing to tell my story, to be heard, to find a voice. After the first draft was complete, I took a copy of the manuscript to my high school history teacher, Mr. Dennis. He was happy to see me and excited to hear of the Navy stories and plans for the future. I gave him a compact disc with the draft on it, shy about the project and cautious about sharing it with anyone. He asked me what my hopes were, and I told him that college wasn't for me and that I was planning to become a commercial diver.

The plan was a patchwork attempt at finding cohesion. After the first year of community college, my grades were the worst of my life. I was out of money and getting into more debt by the day.

After working for a coffee shop for six months and drinking every night, I was financially drained and credit cards became my assistance. I was homesick for the sea, a deep, lonesome hole that drew me to the beach every day, where I handwrote the first draft of my book and chain-smoked out of the open window of my Jeep in the frigid winter. I started looking for a job on boats, quit the coffee job in a petulant burst of reclaiming my freedom, and luckily found a job as a boat detailer within two weeks. The job was physically hard, but it gave me time to think about writing and plan my next move. At the end of summer the boat job dried up and I was back to looking for work. I had landed a seasonal job at an outdoor clothing store, but in January the work dried up. Looking for work again, I found almost nothing. Although I was accepted into dive school, I needed a cosigner for the student loan because the GI Bill didn't cover it. Although I asked everyone in my family to be that cosigner, no one could. I was out of dive school due to insufficient funds. For the first time in my life opportunity seemed to disappear completely, and I saw nowhere to go. I was stuck.

Then the Great Recession hit.

And with it a terrible depression I had never known.

I scavenged job ads compulsively. A temporary job came available, working as a canvasser for an environmental nonprofit. I took it and started immediately with a crew of other young kids who desperately needed work. Most of them were homeless, and they taught me how and when to scavenge food from dumpsters. They were couch-surfing and doing their best not to outstay their welcome at friends' houses. Many of their families had disowned them. So this is where we end up? The things I learned from them—their hardships and struggles, and the dangerous and violent places of their youth—humbled me greatly. Most of them reeked of alcohol. Or was it me?

The job was to stand on street corners and ask people to donate money to the cause. At the beginning of the first day, one of the crew asked someone for a donation and the pedestrian spit in his face. He quit immediately. Only three of us survived that first day. I had to have at least one donation to earn a day's worth of wages, which were minimal. Of the three that survived that first day, I connected with a girl named Lea, and she was somehow capable of smiling even though her gloves had holes and her meager winter coat was soiled and stank. The next day we rode the bus to an affluent grocery store. Her humor and the proximity of her body warmed me. We chose different entrances to the store to maximize our individual contributions. I took the side with a homeless man, who had a bottle of liquor in a brown paper bag and an empty coffee cup in front of him. I mustered the greatest amount of gregariousness I could maintain, swallowed my pride, and asked people for contributions. The abuse was heavy, suffocating. Constant denial with scorn and abusive language made it nearly impossible to keep my resolve.

The homeless man's cup would fill up, he'd dump it into his bag, and it would fill again.

"How can you be getting so much money by just sitting there, and I'm actually working and no one will even talk to me?" I said. The anger spewed out of my voice with the cold vapors of my breath.

"I don't know what to tell you, kid. It's a hard world out here," he said, with a toothless smile.

I made it through the week after completely manipulating conversations with strangers, out of desperation and survival, and Lea was the only other one who made it. I got a full week's pay, and after I received the check I quit.

Bills were paid with credit cards, falling further. I finally got an interview for a dump truck job. At the interview, more than a hundred men lined the walls of the shitty old warehouse in chronic disrepair. I had the first group interview of my life, where men at my side shook with fear. It was a competition and a mind game of survival of the fittest. Every man there needed that job. Many had families, mouths to feed. There were reporters documenting the interview because no one else in the city was hiring. A crummy job interview was a newsworthy event. What the hell was happening?

I reached deep down into myself and found the confident man of military bearing, and I fought through that interview with everything I had. I was one of two men who got a job.

The job was thankless, dirty, and the state of the city was depressing. The recession was eating people alive. The circles I traveled in, people were starving. I returned to the house I shared with Tate, and since he was out to sea on his last deployment, there was no money to heat the house. It was an icebox. I could see my breath as I cooked my daily ration of potatoes. I rationed my money to buy cigarettes and potatoes and attempted to pay bills. That's all I had. Potatoes for months, a sure as hell way to get a six-pack. If I had less pride, I'd dumpster-dive. I modified my cigarette addiction by changing to rolling papers and pouch tobacco because I couldn't afford it.

My family didn't have much money when I was a kid. Where we're from, they weren't called the projects, locals called it the Russian ghetto. Officially, we resided in a Housing and Urban Development Section 8 subsidized housing complex south of Seattle, and the tenants were predominantly immigrants from Russia and Ukraine. Our complex was a large, one-road circle with a little more than a hundred units and only one street to enter. We had a pool and two small parks at the center of the circle. Each of the inner circle's six cul-de-sacs contained twelve townhomes, and the outer ring contained the remainder of the bays. In the second bay on the right, third townhouse on the left, I lived as the second child of a four-sibling family.

In our family and our church, gender roles were strictly upheld. We went to an Independent Fundamental Baptist church, and, trust me, those adjectives were badges of honor to the congregants. Men wore pants. Women wore skirts or dresses. Modesty was the yardstick by which every social choice was measured. Girls had long hair. Most boys had buzz-cut hair. Because of this, my head was buzzed for most of my youth. All the boys in our family wore jeans and white or blue shirts. I was the oldest of three boys, and together we shared one of the three bedrooms in our small townhome. My mother and older sister had long hair and wore oversized jean skirts with white or pink shirts. My mom made oversized dresses for my older sister and herself with her sewing machine. We looked like a uniformed group, and people would glance at us sideways whenever we left the house.

Along with rigid gender roles, we were not allowed any influence from the outside world. The only music we were allowed to listen to was made by traveling evangelists and sounded like old revival music from the nineteenth century. We didn't have cable, and the television was only used for movies that were strictly censored; no sensual content whatsoever, no crude language, no violence or rebellion. We could watch some Hallmark or Disney movies, but our dad had a conspiracy theory about Disney implanting his children's minds with evil, so even those weren't always around. It was a rare thing to have pop culture in the house. In many ways we resided in a cult complex, cut off from the rest of the world.

We went to church twice on Sunday, in the morning and the evening, and on Wednesday night. If my parents were feeling especially pious, we attended a Bible study at church or someone's house on Thursday night. On sunny Saturdays we went door knocking and invited strangers to the Sunday-morning service. Even more than our home, our church was the center of our family. My siblings and I even attended the church's private school when we could afford it, or we were homeschooled. But for two years we were allowed to go to the local elementary school, Camelot, a name that gave me a sense of purpose in life. Lance: a fitting name for a student at a medieval school that emphasized the legends of the Knights of the Round Table. Its stone walls were filled with smooth pebbles of myriad size that I could run my fingers across while daydreaming down hallways that echoed like a castle. I viewed our round housing complex as a stand-in for King Arthur's table, and the school empowered my imagination. I wanted to be an adventurer like the Knights of the Round Table. I wanted to go forth.

My first exposure to gay culture came from that school. My sister's teacher was outed as gay, and a large part of the community of Camelot elementary was up in arms. Our father served as ringleader, saying it was inappropriate that such a person could teach his children. My siblings and I hid on the stairs to eavesdrop on our parents because they were so angry. Mr. Ridley was the most beloved and fun teacher in the school. Our sister loved him. I didn't know what the reason was that he shouldn't be able to teach, but based on my sister's affection for him, I thought it was wrong to try to take his job. I remember that night, when a neighbor babysat us and we waited impatiently as our parents went to the pitchfork meeting. They came back defeated. The school would not fire him for being gay. There were two outcomes of that witch hunt, though. One was that I would not be allowed to be in Mr. Ridley's class next year; I would have another teacher. The other outcome was that I now had a good sense of the very real dangers of being different. While I didn't quite understand the stakes at that time, I was shown that there was real danger when a man loved another man.

In a poignant and perhaps ironic turn of events, the next year in school I auditioned for the role of James in the play *James and the Giant Peach*, under Mr. Ridley's tutelage. I won the role and was happy to have the experience of being the star in his production.

Our church services were a somber affair. Shows of emotion by anyone other than the preacher were contained to a random "Amen" from a congregant moved by the Holy Spirit. We sang songs from ancient hymnals as we stood in front of the pews, with the piano as our only background music. The songs were more spoken than sung, and even the good songs like "Amazing Grace" came off as sad, monotone, compared to the few times I've heard them sung by the secular public. The church believed in the unerring accuracy of the King James Bible as God's literal word and believed that we were to be in the world, not of the world, so a strictly separatist dogma permeated every aspect of our lives.

After a year of homeschooling, my mom found a public school whose student population consisted mostly of prior homeschooled kids from Christian backgrounds. We started attending it the following year.

During a cinema class, Mr. Dennis—one of the new school's nonreligious teachers—brought up a strange part in *Lawrence of Arabia*. It was cryptic. What was he trying to say when he said, "What do you think is going on here?"

Most people didn't notice, but I was accustomed to observation as a means of assimilation and survival. His words were not in tune with the normal narrative of everyday life. I knew something was there. But it was always that way with Mr. Dennis. He went on these big vacations every summer but only came back with pictures of himself. One of our fellow schoolmates once asked the question, "Do you think Mr. Dennis is gay?" and everyone laughed it off. "There's no way that anyone we know is gay," someone said. "Especially not Mr. Dennis. I mean, can you even imagine him dating a woman?" Everyone laughed.

We loved Mr. Dennis. He was a kind man who encouraged greatness in his students. He once said something to me after I haphazardly wrote a paper.

"You have this uncanny ability to write about nothing at all and make it entertaining," he said sternly, as he put the paper on my desk face down. "If you apply yourself, you just might end up being a great writer."

I blushed, that apple-red bloom I so commonly bestowed on anyone who granted me more attention than normal. "I'll try harder next time, sir," I said, guilty in the knowledge that I only used one piece of information that I barely even paid attention to in order to write the two-page paper. When I turned the paper over—an A written at the top—his words were immediately memorialized in the halls of my brain. I'll never forget his belief in my ability.

I began to pay attention. There was truth there somewhere, and I knew someone else had to have taken those pictures all across Europe. I'd imagine who that person could be, content to take the pictures and not be in them. Content to be invisible, silent, nonexistent in the majority of Mr. Dennis's world, at least from our perspective. A deep sadness began to form in me. Hiding was essential. Silence was the only option.

As a child, my mom would bring me grocery shopping with her. She gave me the honor of being her accountant. We were on the lookout for sale items or generic brands, and I used her calculator to keep a running total. As a reward for keeping us under budget, she said I could grab my favorite candy, Starburst. After the attendant rang up the candy, I fingered the foil wrapping and cut through the packaging with my fingernails, my mouth watering. The total rang on the register. My mom pulled out the food stamp checkbooks of varied colors, peeled out each bill from the book with a loud *riiiip*, and counted them out like cash.

She came up short. Her face went flush and so did mine. I scratched at the Starburst repeatedly. The cashier's eyes darted around the store and back to the long line behind us. My mom took items out of the bags that she thought we could live without, item by item. I backed away and set my Starburst down on the bagging station of the aisle next to us.

The lady in line behind my mom quietly said, "I'll take care of it, honey." The three adults did their best to quickly overcome the obstacle that caused their faces to redden and their hands to shake, and then we were out the door. In the car I sat facing the window, hunched over and hiding. My mom put something on my lap and said, "Budgets are hard. We'll figure it out." It was my Starburst with fingernail cuts through the packaging between each individual piece.

Because of her, I learned in my youth how to manage meager resources. Now the rolled cigarettes that stained my fingers were an indictment of my mismanagement of the few resources I had left. I began to ween myself off the nicotine, fighting the urges to use them to salve my feelings of anxiety. It was time to put this terrible habit aside for good.

In the early spring came a faint light of hope from a phone call. The boat company was picking up work, and they needed someone who knew what to do. I took it, part-time as it was, and quit the dump truck job.

I got an email from Mr. Dennis. He read my book and said it was like three different books in one. "What is the story you're trying to tell?" he asked. "You know, a lot of people want to be writers. Maybe you should think about going to school?"

In the haze of being on the fringes, I hadn't thought about tomorrow, hadn't thought of anything other than survival. There it was. Another sliver of shining hope. Because I had an honorable discharge, I still had the GI Bill, and I could go back to school. I could be the first college graduate in my family. Maybe I could follow my childhood dream of being a firefighter. I could get my EMT certification as part of my associate's degree. There were avenues out of this darkness, and I was beginning to chart a new course. Maybe this recession wouldn't kill me.

During the Great Recession, I started over. Again. But now I was armed with a dark experience that propelled me. The first thing was to get back into community college. The boat job gave me the stability I needed to get back in that saddle, so I reenrolled after a year's absence, realizing I had a lot of work to do to make up for the poor grades from my first year. I needed straight A's if I had any chance of getting into the University of Washington. Before, I had been unsure of what I would major in, but now I had a clear direction. I wanted a writing degree and to fulfill my dream of being a writer.

With that outlook, I set my sights on rewriting my book. This time I took Mr. Dennis's prompt and tried to figure out what story I was trying to tell. Now I knew. It was about my experience with Don't Ask, Don't Tell, the scars from it, the triumph over it. I started writing a memoir, trying to come up with an outline and a narrative.

After studying for the test for months, I made it into the EMT course at North Seattle College and began a summer program that took all of my time. I was wholeheartedly dedicated to raising my grades, and during the final year of my associate's degree I made it to the dean's list. Without knowing how difficult it would be to get in, I wrote a vulnerable letter of application to the University of Washington, where I told my story as succinctly and as honestly as possible. There was no back-up school, no back-up plan. In my mind, there was no other option.

News came in the mail one fine summer day. An elegant purple envelope: the University of Washington accepted me! All the work had paid off. After graduating with my associate's degree, I was getting the opportunity to become a first-generation college student and earn a bachelor of arts degree.

At university I plunged into my writing, penning op-eds for the campus magazine and local nonprofits. I even became the editor of the English department's literary magazine, *Bricolage*. I was churning with momentum from everything that was in my rearview mirror, and I was going places. With this newfound determination, I fought a yearslong battle to quit smoking cigarettes. One day I quit for good.

My relationship with my mom had weathered some trying times, but we kept trying to make it through to a place of peace. One day she confided in me that her high school boyfriend had come out as gay. Not long after, he contracted AIDS, dying a few years later. She implored me to understand that she had a difficult time coming to terms with my sexuality because she was afraid I would die young. She viewed being gay as a death sentence. After my experiences in life thus far, I couldn't say she was that far off the mark. My being gay had been a danger on every road I'd walked.

I read a book that shook my core and illuminated the perspective my mom had about my sexuality: *Becoming a Man: Half a Life Story*, by Paul Monette. So little of the book involved the seventeen years of happiness Monette had with his deceased lover, Roger, and there was nothing of the six years without him, in which he wrote the book while he walked alone on the long road of AIDS-related illnesses out of this life. The entire book is the maelstrom of him working toward the point of his "real life." It is utterly heartbreaking, half of his real life of forty-nine years—a bit more than half an expected life span—the first half of his life before he actually felt free. For gay men in America, this half-life is a glass half-empty, one we are forced to drink.

What astounded me was Monette's fury, his anger, with statements like: "And if one of those sick know-nothing bigotries was wrong, then maybe they all were." When I first read this passage, I felt like he was projecting this attitude toward bigots, but I realized that he was attacking a mentality instead of an individual or a community. So much can be learned by calling out the hatred instead of the hater, can be understood by the righteous anger of this man, who weathered so many storms to find a morsel of happiness.

What broke my heart deeply was the fact that he spent all his words on the challenges he faced in finding the thing he sought the most, and so very few sentences immortalizing the found thing. He was constantly searching for his "laughing man." I think that he was looking for this not only in his hopeful lover, but also in becoming such a man himself. It seemed every movement toward this hope was thwarted by himself and society at large.

He was clear in highlighting the "bigotries" he had been wounded by. He named them without subtlety and moved through them with purpose. He knew what had harmed him and was quick to attack it. I wondered how my work could be so focused. How could I speak truth to the powers that have offended me without holding back, as Monette did in his work? I wondered if he only had this power because he was on his deathbed.

What I found most pressing in his words was a palpable anger, something I have shied away from expressing, much less acknowledging, my whole adult life. I've chosen to use my anger to physically propel myself through life. Like another writer, Lidia Yuknavitch, I believe that "there is a way for anger to come out as energy you let loose and away. The trick is to give it form, and not a human target. The trick is to transform rage." Perhaps Monette did this same thing in a different way. I've come to the transformative realization that while he grappled with his tragedies, he transformed them into an ethos for me to confront mine, creating a pathway for people like me to be released from our own chains. What was this laughing man that he speaks of, and where could I find him?

On January 23, 2012, I drove to the United Food and Commercial Workers International Union (UFCW) Local 21, greeted the

Human Rights Campaign (HRC) Team that I'd been working with, and jumped into their SUV. We drove to Olympia and discussed all the latest news on the marriage equality bill. Washington was one vote away from being able to pass the bill in the senate, and the region we had been canvassing the week before was our closest bet to clinching the needed vote. The ferry lines we sifted through had given us ample signatures to send to Senator Mary Margaret, and the experience had also inspired tears from one of us, Rachel, who withstood a brutal verbal beating from a volatile man. The opposition was said to be bringing ten thousand opponents to today's hearing, a number that seemed highly exaggerated, but the intimidating feeling it left was quite indelible. The SUV that carried the four of us was thick with excitement and anxiety. We sweated in our best suits, while someone cracked a window.

When we got to Olympia, I was astounded by the architecture. I grew up in this state, had driven past the capitol innumerable times, and had only seen the building from the highway. The monumental structure and surrounding compound filled me with throbbing anticipation. We entered the building that held the senate hearing and walked through hallways of marbled walls that encased rivers of people, and to our dismay saw many opponents wearing red buttons with silhouettes of one man and one woman. I had a green equality button on my shirt. Their eyes scoped the button, blood filled their pale faces, and they looked up to scan my face with their narrowed eyes. The heat in the hallway rose. I was notified that although the campaign really wanted me to testify, they could only guarantee three people's testimonies; I was not one of them. I felt a bit sore from the letdown. They told me to sign the testifier sheet because after the three, they would be hearing as many people as time allowed.

The halls were a frenzy of chaotic energy, vibrating with the ardent murmurs of so many passions. I was given a video camera and asked to start gathering video testimonies of supporters. With a mission to carry out, I surged through the crowds looking for those friendly pins and found many. Their willingness to tell me their stories filled me with camaraderie, as their stories brought love to my heart and compassion to my eyes. I sifted through the senate floor and the numerous overflow rooms in search of their stories and found them to be as abundant as the red-branded opponents who eyed me and listened to every word from my testifiers' mouths. I smiled and greeted the reds as well. They told me they wanted to testify; they stamped their feet, but I said I had a mission to fulfill and had to continue. There were too many names to recall. There were elderly couples who said if marriage was only about procreation, they wouldn't be allowed to get married. There were parents there who wanted their children to be able to get married. There were interracial couples who said they weren't allowed to get married a few decades ago. There were gay and lesbian couples who wanted to get married for a myriad of reasons. There were kids in high school, middle, and grade school who wanted to grow up and get married to the person they fell in love with. There were union workers, teachers, politicians, state employees, students, clergy and other religious figures, healthcare workers—the list of supporters was unending. I learned so much about my community that I had never known as I asked questions from behind my video camera.

The senate session began and the bill was introduced, followed by the accounts of the designated testifiers. Their stories were a lot like my own.

An opponent, a fundamentalist preacher, heralded his disdain for marriage equality, his outright hatred, and raised his voice to say, "Gays have all the rights they'll ever need already, too many! Why should they start taking ours? Civil unions are separate but equal!"

A Methodist minister stood and said, "Brother, our God teaches of love. And I remember not long ago when the words you used were used to hurt another group of God's children." His voice softened the room.

The testimonies volleyed between supporter and opponent. I waited for my turn, sifting through the past, putting together my monologue, my experiences with inequality. The memory of the court-martial overtook my senses as the faces of the jury haunted my mind. I felt their eyes on me like violent winds and the fury of the JAG officer as he assaulted me with relentless accusations. I wanted to speak for myself, for all the victims of Don't Ask, Don't Tell. I needed to speak for myself, for him, for our love that had been lost, but the hearing ended before I got a chance.

The rooms exploded with people exiting into the bustling halls. I made my way to the pressroom where the campaign was holding a conference. They told me to get video of everything. I made my way to the front of the room with the other journalists. They announced that Senator Mary Margaret had declared her support of the bill. I had a part in that. My HRC group helped make that happen. The crowd erupted in cheers. I looked back to Rachel as she smiled with happy tears. I recalled her face after the verbal battering at the ferry and now saw her transformed before me. It was worth it. It always is. I turned back, as my eyes teared up, and watched history transpire before me through the viewing screen of the camera.

A few weeks later, on February 13, I drove back to Olympia again with my team, this time to watch Governor Chris Gregoire sign marriage equality into law. On the drive up to the capitol, I thanked Adam, the field organizer, for publishing my first essay on a national platform, through the HRC website. The elation of relief I felt for finally getting to speak was beyond expression. He laughed a little and told me that if I did more interviews, I could have a campaign position as field reporter on the team.

So, that is what I did. The legislative building was bursting with people, familiar faces of all those I had interviewed before as well as people from all over the country, there to report and experience such a historical moment under that elaborate domed ceiling. I sifted through the crowds, floating with the sheer joy that echoed through the grand halls, and documented the bliss of all these wonderful people, their families, their stories.

When the doors opened to the state reception room, the designated place of signing, I made my way to the press box and was stopped by the security guard. “Sorry, only people with press passes can enter here,” he said, with diplomatic regard.

I looked around and saw passes from CNN, MSNBC, and various other national and local news agencies. I was well out of my league.

“Oh, I’m sorry. I’m the Human Rights Campaign field reporter. Can I please get through?” I said, with the camera outstretched in lieu of a pass.

The guard gave me a wide, open-mouthed smile, chuckled, and unhooked the satin rope. I was in! I made my way to the front of the press box and knelt down to watch history transpire again before my eyes.

Full Sail and Free

At twenty-seven years old—a U.S. Navy veteran and recent college graduate with a bachelor's degree in writing—I was being evicted from my apartment because the property had been sold to developers. So, I sold or donated 90 percent of my belongings, hoping to buy a sailboat to live on.

At Fishermen's Terminal there was a boat with no name. A retired couple from Canada had donated it to a nonprofit organization in Seattle that raised funds for children's art education. It needed work, but for a 1975 Catalina sailboat, it was in fantastic shape. She was twenty-seven feet long, and I was twenty-seven years old. My boss, Jim, who's taught me everything I know about sailboats, accompanied me to survey it. His recommendation was that it was unlikely I'd find anything better with my budget. I signed the papers and we motored away.

Jim and I made our way through Lake Union's ship canal toward the Ballard Locks. As the waters of the canal receded in luminous green and blue whirlpools and the foaming mouths of the lock's verdigris gates opened, the mooring lines were released, entering the Salish Sea.

We lifted the sails. They were new, with the Canadian maple leaf etched and stitched into the fabric. The wind took us gently into its caress. Full sail. Free. Oh, the dreams I'd had of that moment. Countless days toiling, sweating aboard other people's ships. Days of daydreams of that very moment, when I took my life into my own command. The Puget Sound was wide and far, bordered by the green of forests, spackled by the rustic shades of houses, and crowned by the western range of the Olympics and the Cascades to the east. The Salish Sea: my new home.

We tacked northwest toward Port Madison on Bainbridge Island. The sun burned amber as it sank to rest in the bed of Olympic peaks. The wind fell into slumber. Cirrus clouds shimmered, their sunset shades reflected in the waters below.

Amid these fiery colors, a plop redirected our gaze. To port, another plop, and soon, plops on all sides, a chorus of plops, raindrops of minnows. Rainstorms of fish on all sides as they jumped out and back into the vibrant orange liquid. Splash, from behind us, splash, splash!

All around us, from port to starboard, fore to aft, porpoises jumped, caught, and dove back into the waters. The porpoises looked golden in the feeding opulence. A massive pod, a feasting family. Splash, plop, splash, plop, plop. The porpoises rushed toward the minnows, which dove to survive. Soon the hunters had their fill and the minnows returned to their swimming, and the sun dipped behind the mountains, and the waters went still, and the blue returned, and the lights of the city and the town ignited the encroaching darkness. We lowered our sails and motored toward Shilshole Bay Marina, the resting place of my new ship. I recalled how the dolphins of the Pacific would greet my Navy ship offshore and guide us into ports during deployments. Emissary dolphins: a picturesque and dreamlike ritual that thrilled my young eyes. They had remembered me for this homecoming.

After being greeted by the sea and its creatures in a homecoming greater than any I witnessed in the Navy, for the first time in my life I felt completely independent. In the Navy I was a sailor, part of the crew. That day I became captain. From then on, it was time to solo sail.

Since I'm six foot, three inches tall, the Catalina sloop was barely big enough to live on. If it weren't for my adventure-tinted glasses, I could have viewed my living on a small boat as riding the line of being homeless and living out of my vehicle, but I was enamored with the mystique. I was starting out on my own for the first time and was determined to do it self-sufficiently. No more roommates or people to report to. I was going to direct my own fate, or at least the boat if I could figure out how to operate it.

The learning curve was rigorous. While I had a brief understanding of how to sail, and thought it was a simple affair, it soon became apparent that I had a lot to learn if I wanted to keep the boat afloat.

Once I figured out how to operate the sailboat, I began to build a relationship with the world around me. I measured the responses the boat had to different winds, the way it lurched or smoothly settled. I noticed when the boat felt sturdy and when it felt like it was about to capsize. My attention was wholly on the task at hand, and this turned into a type of meditation for me.

Below, in the small cabin, I had a print of my favorite painting, *The Ship*, by Salvador Dalí. A friend had introduced it to me when I was a teenager, and it had stuck with me like no other painting had. When I lived ashore I had a poster-size print that I spent years staring at, deep into the complexities of a body that was half-human and half-ship, a body that rode the line between two worlds and was nearly lost to both. The tension, and torture, of this individual struck me and continued to command my attention. Now on my own ship, the painting had taken on a whole new meaning. The more I learned how to take care of that vessel, the more I understood that I needed to take care of myself.

As I learned to sail, the lines in my hand began to feel like appendages of my own body. Much like the subject of Dalí's painting, the longer I sailed, the more the boat became a part of me, and with it, the more that I understood my part in the natural environment.

The more balanced my relationship with the boat, the better I moved through the sea. The more balanced my relationship with the environment, the better the ship moved through the region. That knowledge inspired new understandings of my relationship with myself.

Close-hauled and cruising through a moderate breeze, with my rigging tight and trimmed accordingly, I noticed the rigging of my own body, the tension in my neck and shoulders, the pain, steady and constant. Where did this pain come from? Why had I lived with it my entire adult life?

As I'd done when I observed the relationships between me, the boat, and the environment, I began to observe when the pain in my shoulders heightened. This was my body talking to me. I became aware of the thoughts that preceded the pain. I realized that my posture came from decades of habit. As a child, I had been taught that being gay was an abomination, that there was no place for gay people, and I understood that this meant there was no place for a person like me. I moved through the world with self-loathing, my tall frame lowered forward into a posture of acquiescence. This self-talk of self-loathing, instilled in me, wrote itself into my muscle and bone. That philosophy caused me to think myself unworthy to stand up straight, or to be taller than those around me. The rigging of my body had been hunched forward for decades, bowing to my surroundings and the pressures placed upon me.

On the first ship I lived on, as a sailor in the U.S. Navy, I had to fit myself into other small boxes. I was lucky enough to get the top rack in a narrow alley that consisted of bunkbeds stacked three high. There were sixty other bunks in a small room called the berthing. I would lay awake at night, unable to sleep, as I listened to the snoring men who surrounded me and the waves crashing against the hull. I couldn't sleep because I wasn't safe. I had come out as gay under the Don't Ask, Don't Tell policy, and my days there were numbered. The weight of that injustice was being written into my body, and the hunched-forward posture I had grown up with was weighed down by the burden that I carried. The teachings I had been taught as a child—that there was no place for people like me—had now been proven, written into law, and threatened my present and my future. I couldn't stand up straight from the weight of it all. This posture would be with me for years to come.

I lived on that sailboat for six years. Regular maintenance was a requirement, a nonnegotiable aspect of boat life. I had to refill my water tank from a hose on the pier. There was no water if I didn't fill it. When my propane tank ran out, I had to disconnect it and take it to the local boating store to refill it. I couldn't cook on my propane stove if I didn't keep the tank full. There was no bathroom, so I had to ride my bike up the long dock to the community bathroom. If I didn't bring all my toiletries with me, I couldn't brush my teeth, and if I didn't bring two quarters and a towel, I couldn't take a shower. Nothing about living on that boat came easy. It took planning and preparation. It took awareness and work.

The seasons brought different experiences to boat life as well. The summer was truly incredible. I sailed most days of the week, and my friends and family came to enjoy the sun and the wind. Fall brought a chill in the air and a foreboding sense of what lay ahead. I'd sail a few days a week and prepare for the coming storms. The winter brought solitude. No one came to the boat in the cold. I used space heaters and heated blankets to stave off the frigid environment, but the hull emanated the cold water of the sea surrounding me, and the condensation on the hull caused anything made of fabric to get wet, including the edges of my blankets if they touched the bulkheads. The winter was something to endure. It was not pleasant. But then came the spring, the buds on the trees and plants, the warmth in the air. This was the season to open the hatches and let the light in. It was the season of life, a new welcome to get outside and raise the sails.

I learned that to live on a boat meant to take ownership of all your needs. That in turn taught me how to care for myself mentally, physically, and spiritually. Living on a boat taught me to strive for balance. I learned that sailboats cannot sail without the wind, and they need balanced rigging. My life is no different. How can I expect to live if I haven't taken care of myself, if my sails aren't rigged for life? If I don't care for the vessel, it will fall apart. I am no different.

It's taken me a while to learn to stand up straight in the world, and this ability has come from understanding the role self-talk has on my body. When the experiences from my past arise, I assuage myself with the knowledge that the past is the past, and today that reality is not the only reality. There is so much to learn still about how my past has affected my present condition. Sailing has so much more to teach me more about all these relationships. I've come a long way on this voyage, and there's still a long way to go. I'll go farther if I find the right balance between myself, this vessel, and the elements. Sailboat life taught me that.

Solo

The marina is soft, supple in evening tranquility. Sunset is unfolding; now it reclines and reaches its warm autumn arms outward. A visitor's text wakes me from my cockpit meditation.

"I'm here. Come let me in?"

The rehabilitated bike that sits at the end of the dock awaits. I grab it, jump on, and ride the length of the dock to the locked gate. Brock is here, in his holey khaki shorts and black tank top with a brown paper bag tucked under his arm.

"Looks like you're a natural." He nods at the bike, which I dismount. I give him a big hug and he kisses me with hunger. As I walk the bike beside me, we make our way back to the boat. "I still can't believe you made this happen."

"Neither can I," I say, my voice overly eager as I marvel at all the expensive boats we walk past. "Here it is!"

"Where'd you come up with that name?" Brock laughs a hearty heave and points at the name—*Blazin' Guns*—stenciled in Star Wars font on the bow of the boat.

"It was a Navy nickname. For my large . . . personality."

We step aboard and climb down into the boat's interior. There's not much room for the two of us.

My Catalina sloop has both a mainsail and a jib. The hull and keel are in decent shape, but they will need some work in the coming years. The sails are in good condition, but the fiberglass needs some waxing. The canvas cockpit cover, called the bimini, is old and moldy. Some of the stitches have rotted out from exposure to the elements, and the plexiglass windows are scratched and dulled. The woodwork of the entry hatchway is in semidecent condition, and the tiller has been varnished to an extravagant degree. It stands out vividly and makes the rest of the boat look older.

I've already opened the boat for Brock and me to enjoy, but to get into the interior we have to slide the hatch forward and lift two large wooden slabs out of the slots they sit in. Inside is a small wooden ladder with three steps. We step into the cabin. There is less than a hundred square feet of livable space.

In this three-foot-square area are six feet, one inch of standing space in the entry hatchway. We are almost hugging. This is the only standing space in the boat for a six-foot, three-inch man like me, if you can even call it standing. Brock makes it hard to move. To the left is a propane heater that doesn't work. Next to it is a propane stove that does, and beyond that is a small sink with pump handles to produce cold water. To the right, a bench, a table, and another bench. I put the table down to create a bed smaller than a twin. We sit on it. Just behind the ladder on either side are quarter berths: two holes just large enough for a person to climb inside to sleep. They are positioned aft, directly under the cockpit benches outside.

Forward of the main cabin, just past the sink, is what can be considered a small room but is more like half a closet. To the left is a compartment where I hang my few clothes. To the right is a toilet without a storage tank, so the sewage would go right over the side of the boat if I used it, which is illegal in coastal waters. Just forward of this compartment is the V-berth. I have to climb into a three-foot-by-two-foot hole to get into a bed that is four feet wide and tapers to a V that is six inches wide. My feet can cram into the bow of the boat, while my body sleeps in the fetal position in the six-foot-long sleeping space. Brock and I won't fit.

There is woodwork throughout the boat's interior, classical nautical themes, with portholes for windows. The bulkhead lights can be white or red. In every crevice and hole is some sort of compartment for stowing belongings. And that is the extent of my new home.

"It's pretty small," Brock says, and sets his bag down.

"Yeah, but it's beautiful down here, don't you think?"

"Million-dollar view, for sure." He looks around the compartment and pulls out beers from the brown bag, pops the tops of two, and hands me one.

"Guess what? Vashon Island finally called. I start EMT Academy tomorrow! I'll be a volunteer firefighter by next summer."

"Fantastic!" Brock says. He embraces me, kisses my neck, wrestles me down to the floorboards. "Sexy fireman. I can't wait for that uniform."

I pull some pillows down from the bed to get comfortable. "Don't get ahead of yourself, officer. I have a long way to go."

I recall meeting him those many years ago, our dates while he was on shift in his squad car at the top of that parking garage overlooking Seattle. I'd get us coffees, drive my car to our rendezvous spot, and have them ready for him whenever he was between calls. "I don't think I've ever seen you in uniform outside of work anyway."

"I've been saving that for when you become a firefighter," he says. A grin ignites his face. A stereotypical porn fantasy, a fireman and a cop.

We drink a few celebratory beers as the waves rock the boat.

"I like the way it moves. It's so peaceful here," Brock says, leaning against my chest.

"Wait until you sleep over. It's like a baby being rocked to sleep."

"I bet." He pauses, flicks the edges of his fingernails. "Have you thought about how you'll handle the fire department?"

"What do you mean?"

"I've talked to people at my precinct and at Seattle Fire. I know you're planning on applying for the next round of hiring, but as far as I can tell there are no openly gay firemen. You've been really open with your life. Maybe you should play it safe for a while?" He sits up, separates most of his body from mine.

"I'm past all that."

"Look, Lance, you need to take care of yourself. The fire service isn't a very open-minded place. People like us need to be careful."

"I get that. But I can't go back to being silent."

"Maybe you need to."

"But you're out at your job. Don't tell me that the fire service is worse than the Seattle Police Department."

"It took me five years to tell my work partner. Most people still don't know. I'm telling you, buddy, you need to watch your back."

I sit up and back away. The world is feeling that way again, claustrophobic. My lungs constrict as I cough out a reply. "I won't lie anymore. I've come too far. Sacrificed too much."

"You're not being logical about this. Your career is more important."

"You've played it safe. I haven't had that luxury."

He crosses his arms over his chest. "You can now." His face goes softly white. He stops. The only sound is the hollow wind through the sailboat and then his whisper: "I can't go on this journey with you."

I turn away. He doesn't say a word as he gets up and leaves. For the past few years, I've hoped that things between us would turn into something serious. After these handful of on-again, off-again periods, after so many repetitive letdowns, I'm over it. He won't be spending any nights here.

Nightmares of being rejected by the fire service wake me with the howling wind throughout the night.

Drill School

For two years, I lived on the sailboat, worked as a boat detailer, and commuted to Vashon Island to work as a volunteer firefighter/EMT on the evenings and weekends. It was a grueling schedule but gave me the edge I needed to rank high on the Seattle Fire Department registry, compiled from thousands of competitive applicants from all over the country. To my surprise and pleasure, and with the help of my veteran's service credit, I ranked eleven on a list of finalists and was offered a job in the first class hired from that list.

In summer of 2014 drill school begins. Our first week is in preparation for the chaos to come. It proves to me that all the work I did as a volunteer at Vashon Island Fire and Rescue these past two years was useful. I know the basics of donning my bunker gear in under a minute, throwing on my self-contained breathing apparatus (SCBA) in under a minute, what the gear I use is, and how it works. That's a leg up on some of my fellow recruits with no experience at all.

The second week begins the major segment of drill school, called the Grind. This six-week chunk of training is when we prove to the instructors that we are physically capable of doing the job. From Monday to Thursday we are drilled in preparation for a test on Friday. We must pass the test each week, and if we fail we're given one retest. Any retest looks incredibly bad. If for some reason we fail that retest, we are placed on conditional employment. If we fail a second drill, we are fired. The stakes are high; we have to earn our jobs. Nothing is guaranteed at this point. These are tryouts.

In the chaos of instructors screaming, while I am trying to focus on using the engine's hydraulic system to pump water to the hose lines, I'm reminded of Michael Sam, who has recently come out during the NFL draft. The historic kiss with his boyfriend on ESPN was a bold move. Being the first openly gay man to attempt to get into the NFL has caused a frenzy of reporting and speculation. For me, Sam is a social experiment with huge implications for my life. I too am trying to make the cut of a team that, as far as I know, has never had a man like me on it. I've been watching to see the outcome of his bold attempt. He's just been cut from the Rams, and that blow to his life reverberates in mine. His unknown future reflects mine and that of so many others. Can we be open? It seems to have cost him his career already. When Sam played in college he was out to his team, which is a huge reason he came out to the media—because everyone already knew. Like Sam and his teammates, two people from Vashon Island Fire and Rescue got hired with me in this class. They know me and know I'm open. I guess the best I can do is manage how much attention that gets, if I can manage it at all. Michael Sam couldn't. It's not readily apparent that I'm gay, so I'm sort of always in the closet if I'm not open. So, the questions are, Can I be silent, and Will my friends talk? I decide to be strategically silent. I'll choose my battles and keep my private life out of it.

"Recruit, what the hell are you doing?" An instructor attacks my left ear with heated words. My immediate thought is that he could tell what I was thinking. It's obvious that I'm a homo. Everyone knows. I'm totally fucked.

"Send them water now!" I hadn't noticed in my fearful reverie that I wasn't doing my job fully. I focus intently on finishing my task, and in less than a second I'm done. The instructor runs off to yell at someone else as I review my steps and focus only on the present moment. This engine is confusing, so many levers and gears, so many steps, and I'm required to know all of them already with no prior experience of what they are, much less how they operate. In a training regime with little time for such inaccuracies, this process is going to be full of mistakes. I must perfect this process and three others before Friday in order to pass. The learning curve is a sheer cliff, and we are required to climb it without fear or hesitation.

I remember the gun mount in the Navy, the foreign systems that in the beginning were difficult to master, but how I learned them and became a good technician. That experience qualifies me here.

The days go by in a flurry. The screaming instructors make me feel like I'm back in Navy Special Warfare training. Somehow, I feel like I'm in the same place I started. Here at drill school, maybe I can find atonement from my failure at SEAL training. I will get redemption for that failure. Those days of abuse on the sands of Coronado have prepared me for the abuse on this concrete training facility. How uncanny that this part of training is called the Grind. As I run up and down the six-story concrete tower, I recall the Grinder of SEAL training, the concrete pavilion that was used to drill us into failure. The Grinder and the Grind. I've got it this time.

Decked out in full bunker gear and riddled with sweat and exhaustion, I run the tower. After my experience at SEAL training, I discovered Brett Jones's book about when he was outed while he was a Navy SEAL in 2003, which was a few years before I showed up for training. In hindsight, I know that those days when I felt like I was being smoked out, being warned that it wasn't okay to be gay in their ranks, were justified. While Jones said that he found some support from his SEAL brethren, it didn't change the fact that his career was on the line from the moment he was exposed. Like me, Jones got out with an honorable discharge; we both were motivated to leave on our own terms after we were outed, before we were kicked out. But he went the distance and became a SEAL. I didn't. Regardless, he wasn't allowed to be open. He had to live in the shadows. That haunts me as I climb these concrete steps. No matter what happens this time around, no matter what challenges come my way, I will go the distance. Brett Jones gives me strength. Michael Sam gives me hope. The injustice charges my resolve. My legs are fired up with the passion of overcoming the obstacles in our way. I run the stairs again and again. I do the drills. I grind the Grind.

As the days of the first weeks go by, we use the engine's hydraulic system to charge the lines, take hoses into simulated burning buildings, run stairs, and do it all over again. The instructors yell. The mechanical sounds of the engine, the roar of the water flow, the howling of recruits trying their best to communicate amid such chaos, all these sounds create a battlefield of noise. Our bodies strain to save lives. Our minds challenge us to stay motivated. Breathless and spent, we push further still, under strict time constraints and with our careers on the line at every step.

At night, I greet the darkened marina, thankful for the peace of its repose. When I get out of the car, the tranquil waters restore a sense of calm in my raw nerves. The first thing to do is take a shower at the marina. For the better part of these years on the boat, I'd shower at the gym to avoid the situation. It's difficult to bend over and take off my boots in this tiny room. My body aches already, and the work it requires to undress in such a tight space is starting to make me angry. This is a hardship. Before the start of drill school, the lead instructor advised me that I shouldn't be living on a sailboat during training. But this is my life, and it's what I have to work with.

As I labor to take off my boots, I discover blood-drenched socks. Broken blisters afflict me from the boots I was just issued and didn't have time to break in. They sting as I climb into the two quarters' worth of hot water. Blood mixes with the water and spirals into the drain at my feet.

Afterward, I put some clean clothes back on but fail to keep them dry, because I can't keep them off the wet floor of the shower closet. I make my way down the long dock and clamber into my boat. I'm beyond exhaustion and savagely hungry. Inside, the two dorm-style refrigerators are packed with food that my best friend, Carina, cooked for me. Thank God for Carina. I'm supposed to be on a 10,000-calorie diet to give my body what it needs for training, so I eat a kale salad loaded with calories as the fettuccine alfredo reheats in the microwave on the table. There is no room in this boat anymore. There wasn't room before this voyage started. I stuff my face as I look at the piles of gear I have crammed into every available space. With mouthfuls of food, I pack my bag for tomorrow: new uniforms from the piles of fresh clothes, sandwiches from the refrigerator, new bags of trail mix and dried mangoes from grocery bags under the table, fresh socks and underwear. After the bag is packed and the kale salad is eaten, I pull out the pasta and stuff my face again. As I gorge on the carbohydrates, I pull out my homework to study. There isn't time to do each task one by one.

In a haze now, and close to passing out, I coat my sore muscles with Tiger Balm, that wonderfully fragrant salve which relaxes my muscles. In the narrow passageway of the boat, I begin my evening stretches as my muscles feel the heat from the ointment. Turning the cabin lights from white to red slows the pace of day. I practice breathing, deep, releasing the tension from my muscles. What a day, a week. Tomorrow is finals, for this week at least. I exhale slowly and imagine myself passing the tests, step by step, envisioning my success. Every muscle of my body is stretched, focusing on the trouble spots of my neck and right shoulder, which are wrenched tight and need a lot of work. I've scheduled a weekly massage, as recommended from training, and look forward to it on Sunday. My muscles need it. The salve is heating up as I go over the events of the day, what I did right and where I went wrong. It seems like every time I think about the odds against me, every time I think of how hard it is for gay people, I make a mistake.

As I breathe in deeply, stretching and meditating, I decide that if I'm going to survive this, I must let go of the past. Who knows if I'll be successful, but I do know that constantly reminding myself of the odds against me makes it harder. Here on the floorboards of my boat, I accept that I cannot change the past, and can't change the odds against me, but what I can do is not let that hold me down any more than it does already, if I can move past it.

My biggest challenge is not a physical drill, but a social misunderstanding. I make a mistake when I'm pumping the engine, and a hose that isn't supposed to fill with water expands in the bed of the engine. I push the valve with all my might, but the water still comes. An instructor comes up to me, and I try to explain to him what happened.

"I accidently opened the valve but closed it right after I figured it out. But the water is still coming, and I can't shut it off. It might be broken, or maybe someone before me broke the valve. I don't know what happened."

I was trying to troubleshoot the problem with him, but he thought I was coming up with excuses and not taking ownership. He doesn't say as much at that moment, but within fifteen minutes the lead instructor comes up to me, pulls me aside, and starts screaming in my face.

"Your instructor tells me that you're a liar! Why are you lying? We won't let liars be on our team! Are you a liar, recruit?"

"No, sir," I say, without understanding what he is talking about.

He commands me to explain myself, so I tell him the same thing I told the other instructor, that I made a mistake and opened the wrong valve but closed it and the water still kept coming. I tell him how I was trying to troubleshoot the problem and figure it out. His face goes limp, almost apologetic, before he raises his voice again and screams that we can't have liars in the department so make sure this never happens again.

I find the instructor I had initially talked to about the problem, apologize for any confusion, and tell him my integrity means everything to me. He looks at me skeptically but accepts my apology.

The next few weeks I'm riddled with doubt. My recruit buddy says it must be personal. Is it? Do they not like me already? I become a target for the instructors. Everyone knows me now, and they're just waiting for me to make a similar mistake. At one point they suspect I could be the culprit for another mistake that no one owns up to. I assure them that it wasn't me, that I would own up to it if it was, but the culprit never comes forward, so the mystery of the class liar is pinned on me. I take it personally but try to convince myself that everything will be fine in the end.

The first six weeks of the Grind are gruesome. Our bodies are overextended, muscles on the brink of strain, our feet and hands blistered and cut. The drills rotate back and forth from engine drills with hose handling and pump operations, to truck drills with ladders and chainsaws. The truck drills revolve around brute strength. We put twenty-four-foot extension ladders on our shoulders and sprint to a building, throw the ladders up, and extend the fly into the window, all in a strict time frame and with no room for error. The drill becomes a competition for the fastest and strongest. We shave off every last millisecond of time that we can, continually challenging each other to be better, to be the best.

We extend thirty-five-foot ladders with tired hands that can barely contain a grip. We must raise the ladder in seconds, and we race each other for the best time. Then we climb the ladders and start cutting holes in pitched roofs. Since I've done this before on the island, I feel a bit more comfortable in this drill.

There is a list of knots that we must tie within seconds. I've had enough experience with knots to pass these tests without a problem, but others are not so lucky. There is no time to make a mistake in the few seconds we have to tie them, so when a mistake is made, it's easy to get frustrated and fail.

One of the hardest drills is to pull a dummy up a flight of stairs in the dark, after refilling its air bottle. No one knows exactly how much the dummy weighs, but it's rumored to be 180 pounds, heavier than me. The drill is timed, which adds even more difficulty because it's hard to feel the hose connections with the thick firefighting gloves we wear. It's pitch-black inside. We stand outside a door and are notified via radio that there is a downed firefighter in the basement. Once we receive the dispatch, we open the door, close it behind us, and do a wall search until we find the limp body, which is lying face down. Once we find the air cylinder on their back, we feel for the hose connection with one hand while pulling out the trans-fill hose from the pouch on their waist with the other. We then uncoil the hose, find the coupling on it, and bring it to the coupling at the base of the bottle. With any luck we connect the two quickly, but often we fumble for the connection, wasting precious time. After the connection, the air equalizes between the two tanks in a loud pressure exchange, the signal that we're ready to pull the dummy up the stairs.

Everyone has a method that they think is the easiest. Some people have to go step by step, doing a backward squat lift at every ledge as they raise the body with both hands, grasping the shoulder straps of the dummy's air pack and making sure the cylinder clears the sharp angles of each step. The stairs prove to be the biggest obstacle, constantly snagging the cylinder and bringing the enormous effort of lifting the dummy to a clamoring halt. My strategy is to grab the shoulder straps of the air bottle with one hand and pull the dummy as I move forward, grab the handrail, and pull upward. I'm the only one who does this method, but it works for me because of my height, and I make it pretty darn close to the fastest time of the group.

It takes a beastly effort to pull the dummy up the two sets of stairs. The landing between the sets is the hardest part because it stops our momentum and forces us to swing the dummy all the way around the landing and change directions. By this point I've completely lost my breath, sucking greedily at the air bottle, unable to get the air to the base of my lungs where I need it the most. My bunker gear is toxically heated, and I panic with the need to rip it all off. But I must continue, so I spin the dummy, swallow my pain, and yank the dummy with all my might up the last flight. At the top of the stairs, we must spin the dummy once more and pull it five feet into the safety of a room. Once in the room I fall backward with exhaustion, totally spent, and rip off my mask to breathe the stale air of the damp concrete building.

"Time is fifty-six seconds. Nice job, recruit." That's the first nice thing an instructor has said to me so far. I can't believe it. That felt like minutes. It felt like I failed the drill. That success fuels my drive to win.

I decide to push for a class record. There are only a few timed drills left before midterms, so if I'm going to get a record, I had better do it quick. In the mornings before drill school, I listen to music to pump myself up for the day as I eat my breakfast. Macklemore's "Make the Money" rings true to me as the lyrics "Change the game, don't let the game change you" run on repeat in my head.

It's a downpour of a day in Seattle. The morning commute highlights what the day will bring for us. Once training starts, the rain adds a whole new dimension. The water adds pounds of weight to our soaking gear. Everything is slowed down. Before the rain, our bunker gear and air pack add fifty-plus pounds to our backs. With the rain, we estimate that it's at least another fifty pounds more. For a dude that started training weighing a buck seventy-five, I must weigh three hundred pounds with all this additional gear. We laugh about it to keep our spirits high, saying we should have lost some weight if we ever wanted to pass this training. A few too many donuts here, and don't forget the carton of ice cream, and that cake! Michelin men on a mission.

The day is miserable, and it's only Tuesday. We have three more days of this. Today's big drill is a standpipe hookup from hydrant to engine to high-rise building. It's the longest drill we will have to do, and doing it in the rain it makes it difficult. My turn comes and I jump up on the engine. With the stopwatch held high the instructor says, "Gooo!" and I begin the complicated step-by-step drill. Change the game. Don't let the game change you. I pump myself up with the song that I repeat over and over in my head, as I lose myself to the movements of my body, forgetting to think and simply floating through the drill. I grab the hose off the back of the engine and run full throttle to the hydrant, but where other people simply drop the hose and turn around, I grab hold of the light pole next to it and use it to catapult myself around and back in the direction of the engine, losing no momentum and actually gaining some.

Change the game. Don't let the game change you. I sprint back and forth, connecting the hoses to the engine, hydrant, and to the standpipe of the high-rise. I'm almost done. My crew is cheering; they can't believe how fast I'm going. I run back to the engine and slip on the wet pavement but catch myself from falling in an almost whimsical dance move before jumping up on the engine and ending the drill.

"Holy shit, Lance, what kind of food are you eating!?" the instructor mutters in disbelief.

"You run like a cantaloupe!" a recruit says, and chuckles.

"An antelope, you idiot," another says to eruptions of laughter. "More like a giraffe, I'd say."

"A giraffe." I laugh and wipe the sweat from my face.

"Definitely a giraffe with those long-ass legs."

"The best part was those stripper moves," the instructor says, and starts to bellow. "I mean, you spun off that pole better than any stripper I've ever seen! The flexibility!"

"Well, if you don't make it through drill school, at least you know you'll succeed in another career," a recruit chimes in. We all roll in a wave of laughter, shedding the weight of the rain and the severe nature of drill school. This is a first: an instructor making jokes and laughing with us. It feels good, but part of me wonders if the stripper joke has to do with my sexuality. I shrug it off. Recently the class leader has taken to calling me Mrs. Williams, because that's one of my teammates from Vashon Island's last name, and we're often on the same team. He even goes so far as to say "Mrs. Williams" in the marching cadence we sing across the compound. The whole class sings it and laughs. He keeps using the joke. I gladly take the Mrs. title because I feel bad for Williams and don't want him to have gay jokes made at his expense. I own it, and we all laugh. Williams knows I'm gay, but does everyone else? Even the instructors? One of the recruits calls us the ambiguously gay duo, and that one strikes closer to a slur. He tries to rattle my bones a bit, but I don't let him. Williams seems unfazed.

Then another recruit calls me "fag."

I turn to him, imposing my towering frame over his five-foot-eight structure, and I respond, "How about you call me something

I haven't heard before?" It's a challenge and also my way of coming out to him. From that point on, I decide to stop being silent. One of the female recruits in our class witnesses the whole thing. After I call him out, I see a gleeful smile on her face. I'll later find out that she is a proud lesbian and was showing solidarity.

It turns out that I made the fastest time on the standpipe drill. The whole class talks about it, laughing about my stripper moves and challenging others to break the record. The next few days are sunny, our gear lighter without the rain. Try as they might, though, no one even comes close to my time. Lauds turn to disbelief when people can't catch up, and some even try to say the time was a mistake of the clock, but the instructor who timed me stands by his account, and I have myself a shiny new class record at the end of the week.

A Friday ritual in drill school, going back generations, is to go to the Siren tavern in the South of Downtown (SODO) district and eat nachos and drink beer, celebrating another successful week. Firefighters from across the city show up to share stories with us as they give their best advice for the coming week. It's a grand tradition at a dingy dive bar, a perfect place for the ruckus of our group.

The remaining weeks go by, and soon we are preparing for midterms. My weekends are usually full with preparations for the coming week, laundry, a massage, stretches, and lots of sleep.

I feel lighter after having faced the terror of the instructors, the accusations, the jokes, and rising above all that to grasp a class record. When midterm week comes into full force, I've come to terms with the chaos of my nerves and the challenges I face. Day after day we are tested on all the drills we have done up to this point. Engine drills of hose handling and pump operations, truck drills of ladder throwing and chainsaw handling, dummy drags and knot tying. I almost fail the final dummy drag after it gets caught on the stair, but somehow, I overcome the challenge. I pass, a perfect score with no failure evolutions. Only a few of us do that. Most of the class fails at least one drill, and some fail their retest, which puts them on the chopping block. A handful of classmates get fired. Midterm week ends, completing the Grind. I'm relieved to be done with what they say is the hardest part of training, and somehow amid the obstacles I've come out in the top percentage of the class, with a perfect midterm score and a class record.

As the second phase of training starts, a fellow recruit searches for me online and finds my self-published book. He starts conversations during drills about my personal life. He tries to be discreet, but you can't hide anything from anyone when you're working in such close quarters. I start to open up, accepting the fact that information like this travels fast.

Curious about the history of gay people in the Seattle Fire Department, I do some research and find little. It will be a few years before I learn about Susi Rosenthal, one of the first lesbian women in the department who ultimately went on to become the first female assistant chief. There is nothing about her online.

But I do find articles about the first woman to serve as a firefighter in the department, Bonnie Beers. She began her career in 1977 and came into a firehouse culture that didn't have female bathrooms. Some women would use utility sinks when no one was around. Beers said she would only shower at home. It was a culture where women had to become "one of the guys" and seldom worked with other female firefighters. The environment was so unwelcoming that if they got pregnant, they could be placed off work for a year without pay or benefits and lose seniority when they returned. Beers retired as a battalion chief in 2008 and was asked by a local LGBTQ+ newspaper what our community can expect if they want to be firefighters.

"She briefly shared a story of a Gay firefighter who was outed in recruit class and ended up quitting to avoid dealing with the fallout. 'Being a recruit is already hard enough without dealing with that dimension,' she said. 'I'm not saying it's impossible, but you'd have to have your shit together.'...Unique in her experiences in an intensely male-dominated, hyper-masculine field, [she] offered advice to Gay firefighters, whether new recruits or veterans: 'If he felt he was accepted enough and he wanted to come out, go ahead! I think it would cause some bumps, but if you're strong and you know what you're doing, go ahead—though if you're having problems or your life isn't exactly right, why would you do that to yourself?' [She] paused. 'I'm sure Gay men are going to have a hell of a time.'"

All of a sudden I feel suffocated, as if the thick smoke inside the house we're burning down for training is surrounding me, like it's Don't Ask, Don't Tell all over. I feel unprotected from the danger, with everything on the line. Again.

Drill school is hard enough without this element. The day after I read the article, I make a major mistake. The instructors hammer me with threats and tell me I could get cut from training.

Then, with only a few weeks to go, I injure my wrist. The instructors make me go to the hospital. The X-ray doesn't show anything, so they tell me I need an MRI, but I beg the doctor to let me finish. I could lose everything if he doesn't let me. He makes me promise him that I will take care of the wrist after I graduate. I promise. Thank God it's Friday. I have the weekend to mull it over and try to heal up. I don't know how the hell I'm going to do this. Finals week is two weeks away. It all comes down to this, and I only have one good hand.

I manage to get through the week before finals week with my hand wrapped with sport tape and Ace bandages. Every night I ice my hand in the frigid waters next to my boat, asking the sea to heal me. Every morning, I wake to intense pain and wrap the wrist as tightly as I can to stabilize it, swallowing ibuprofen like candy. Every day is just a precursor for what is to come. Friday. The true test of my grit will be Friday.

Twenty-six logs sit in a large circle on the concrete. Twenty-six stumps with our names spray-painted in bright orange on the inner rings of the rounds. The logs represent our chance to belong. Twenty-six of us, dull ax in hand, waiting for the starting whistle.

Chainsaw appreciation, meant to ingrain in us how tough the firefighters of the past were. They didn't have chainsaws. It's a rite of passage that every firefighter must accomplish to join the rank and file. I look to my left, where the six-story tower looms over us. In it, the stairs we've climbed day after day, our bunker gear soaked through, hose bundles on our shoulders in stacks of two-hundred-foot sections, the smell of moldy concrete from the dark halls we climb. Opposite the tower stands the burn building, the single-family residence we fight fire in, where we learn how to handle the charged lines, maneuvering through the sharp turns of hallways, deep into the high-heat conditions where victims await us. In the middle of these two buildings, the instructors guide us to our starting positions.

"How's the hand doing?" an instructor asks, his voice softer than the usual authoritative tone.

"It's going to have to do, sir." I'll find out in a few weeks that I've broken the scaphoid bone in my right hand. They'll drill an inch-long screw into it as I watch on the X-ray screen. But I know already that there's something wrong. I felt it last week when I swung the metal Halligan tool like a baseball bat—leading with the pointed adze—and struck the metal door to break it open, sending a metallic rush of pain through my hand. That same moment repeated over and over, for hours. I tried to look like I wasn't injured as we took turns perfecting the art of forcible entry, and all the while the cracked bone collided again and again with the Halligan and the door, causing further trauma.

Classmates talk about strategies against the logs. They practice swinging their axes while I stand with my left hand on mine, like a crutch, trying to learn from them without moving or wasting my energy. Only a few classmates have ever cut through a whole log before. There's a prior lumberjack in the class, and I notice that his stump is the second largest. The idea is to cut at angles, create a wide V at the top of the log and work your way down to the middle, then turn the log over to come at it from both sides. Meet in the middle. Easy enough.

Training started in August. Now the November chill sets in, and a late fall wind blows through the clasps of my bunker jacket, providing a welcome respite after these last months of heat inside our gear. The leaves have mostly fallen to the concrete training ground. I'll be thirty next month. I think about what brought me here, about the seven years I've spent out of the Navy, after my four-year enlistment. I think of the court-martial and Don't Ask, Don't Tell. Seven years since I left the military. Seven years looking for a place to belong, leading to this moment.

The instructors direct us to take our places.

"On my mark," an instructor bellows while the others laugh. "Go!"

We begin the long slog. I swing the ax up over my head, slide my hands together at the base, and launch the blade down to my target. *Thump!*

That initial metallic vibration of the blade colliding with the wood round shudders my injured right hand. I feel the throb of jagged bone.

The instructors, and even the chief, look directly at me, searching.

This isn't the first time I've tried to be a part of a group where there were no others like me, let alone one involving a log. SEAL training. We ran the beach, six of us to a log, up and down sand dunes until we'd all but collapsed with fatigue. I learned there what it meant to push past your boundaries. I learned from Victor Frankl, his words, "Life is potentially meaningful under any conditions, even those which are most miserable." As we suffered together, a class of SEAL candidates, I was keenly aware of my divergence.

In the circle of firefighting recruits I stand, a man trying to fit into the ranks of those who know of my difference, this time trying to be the first openly gay man to do so. And my wrist, unbelievably, cruelly, even comedically, falls limp.

Chunks of sawdust fly around the circle, sticking to the sweat on my face. I think about the instructor who'd just asked about my hand, how days earlier he'd pulled me aside and said, "Don't let someone else make this decision for you. There's no way to know what will happen if you give up your right to choose."

As the hollow chunks of dull metal on wood reverberate around the circle, each strike leaves me further behind. With the ax handle resting on the forearm of my injured right hand, I raise the ax up to my chest. All around me, classmates chop away.

I fill my lungs and heave the ax with all my might high overhead. It crashes down with all the power I can command with my single left hand.

I'm sick of this fear. I'm sick to death of this internal battle. In the circle around me, fellow recruits chop away. I am no less capable than they are. I've proven as much, at least to myself, during this long and arduous training. This will not defeat me. A broken hand will not stand in my way of breaking through. I will be a Seattle firefighter.

With each lift over my head, the ax seems to grow heavier, and I have to focus harder on the downward swing to hit the targeted segment. The left swing is more natural, with me being left-handed, but on the opposite swing—the part that is vital to getting a good v-cut in the wood—it's incredibly awkward. I use the entire frame of my body, twisting my torso out to the right and quickly back to the left at the last second. Exhausted by the effort, I'm only an inch into the wood.

Everything's on the line; I have nowhere to run. But I'm done with running. This is my chance to finally claim my place in the world. I gather my strength with each swing. Every chunk of flying wood is proof that I am capable. Even with one hand. I am emboldened, giddy with stamina. You are a fucking badass, Lance, I tell myself. But each chop ignites sharp pain in my wrist, and with each pang, the epithets slung at me come screaming back: *homo, faggot, abomination*. I fight against them and embrace the pain. Yeah, I broke the most ironic bone in my gay body. Limp wrist. Let me show you what I can do with a limp wrist.

I find a rhythm. I find the beat, and my feet grow light, and my mind flies free. I've found the sweet spot, and I start to sing to myself.

Roll the log over, and over again, over and over, again and again. Chop, chop, swing. Left-handed supreme. Chop, chop, swing. Nothing on me.

The first few classmates make it through their logs. Their battle cries give me momentum. I'm accustomed to being at the front of the pack, so I strive, push, propel myself forward, through the seething muscles of my body and the throbbing, aching bitterness of my bones. I can see the inner rings of the log. They cut closer and closer. I don't give a damn about what's happened before, about my injuries and my scars, about the dangers and the odds against me, about the fact that I'm the first one of my kind to be here, openly, right now. There's just this ax, this log, and me, and I'm about to break through one of the final challenges. I'm about to finish this rite of passage before most of my class. I'm about to—*Clink!*

The ax breaks through the wood and drives into the concrete.

RAAAAAAAWWWWWWWRRRRRRR!!!!!!

My arms drop outward and my chest rises to the sky, my whole body rigid with triumph. After an incredible noise rises from my lungs, I sit on the log I just halved, raise the handle of the ax and rest my helmet on that glorious crutch.

In truly poetic fashion, I rank eleventh out of twenty-six. I ranked eleventh to get this job. Beautiful serendipity.

As they send us home for the last weekend before finals week, they pat me on the back and congratulate all of us for a job well done. I forget about the fears that held me back and even propelled me forward. Something different grows inside me. Is it a healing? I don't know, but I feel renewed.

Every drill we have done for the past sixteen weeks is combined into scenarios that are as close to real life as possible. We are separated into engines and trucks for multicompany operations and have to switch apparatuses after each drill. We must prove that we are capable of doing every drill we have ever been taught, doing it on the fly and without warning, and doing it flawlessly. We are still being graded for every step, and they admonish us, "We've fired people during the last week of training before. We won't hesitate to do it again. Lives are on the line."

My crew asks about my hand. I say I'll make it work. I did last week. They tell me that if I feel like I can't make it, tell them and they will help me out. "We're a team," they say, without wavering. Their support calms my fears.

We ride the rigs, lights and sirens, using the radio to respond to the scene. Smoke billows out of the high tower.

"Patients are trapped." The ominous radio incites us to action.

We jump out of the engine. I grab the hose bundle, put it on my shoulder, and make my way to the entrance of the building, flaking the hose out behind me as I go. After I lay the hose down for easy access to the building's interior, I drop to my knees and put my facepiece on, connect it to air, and call for water. The hard part is putting my right glove on. It doesn't seem to fit, so I have to force it in. The pain is as sharp as the bone in my hand; it travels through my body, to my gut, and makes me gag. I open the nozzle and water comes, and I head into the building.

At the seat of the fire my partner and I stop. We flow water until the first truck company does a search and finds the victim, the second truck company cuts the roof open for ventilation, another engine company gets another backup hose line into the building. There's a truck company in the back of the building doing forcible entry with rescue saws. Another group is throwing ladders into second- and third-floor windows. Yet another is providing box fan ventilation to clear the space of smoke. A victim is rescued. Another. The building changes and the priorities do too. Single-family residences, commercial buildings, apartments, hazardous materials, fire, smoke, victims trapped. The drills keep coming. The noise is deafening. Chainsaws screaming, water rushing, people yelling, motors and fans, metal being cut through, tools banging against metal doors, heartbeats racing, and radios scratching through the ruckus.

For the majority of the drills, I forget that I am doing them one-handed, except for when I put on my glove. Then, as my partner and I begin to put up the thirty-five-foot ladder to floor three, I use my right hand to steady the beam, and my hand violently jerks away like I put my hand in a fire. The weight of the ladder comes back at me. My hand goes back to stop the ladder from falling, but it feels like a spike of bone pushes toward the unforgiving rigidity of the metal, and I cannot hold it. My partner gasps. I'm about to drop our biggest ladder, and the chief is looking straight at us. He will fire me. With all my power I dive under the weight of the ladder, put my left hand next to my fragile right, and push upward against the weight and the violent expanding pain, pushing with the belief that there is a way to overcome the challenges and the wounds and the disasters that affront us. With all that teeming passion and pain I push the ladder high overhead, set the ladder, and climb up and into the dragon's lair.

The final days turn dark and merge into one another. Soon, in the flurry of evolutions and tireless pace, Friday evening arrives. It rains as the last evolution begins. The concrete reflects the red lights, and the weight of our gear doubles with the wetness. Somehow the noise doesn't register. We have grown accustomed to the chaos. We've found the silence in the storm, the eye where we see clearly the task at hand. We see the victim, the whole picture, how to extricate her, how to rescue him, how to defeat the dragon, to do so as one large team built on trust and the knowledge that we all stand here together, fighting for each other, for the cause, for the people we swear to protect. In the dark and glimmering night, we rise from the shadows and emerge as members of an elite force. The evolution is over. We are Seattle firefighters.

I sit on the tailboard of the engine, taking a quick break before cleaning up all the gear. My hand, throbbing, rests open on my right thigh. I don't want to take it out of the glove. Bunker gear is drenched. Sweat runs down my face. I open my coat to let some cool air in to my overheated body.

Tears well up as I sit in the dark. I fight them back, though I don't want to. They are triumphant tears. They have been earned. I've done it. Here, injured and tired, I have risen from the ashes of the past. I have faced the dragon fire of my fears. I have become the first to cross this threshold somehow, survived to tell the tale. As I sit on this tailboard and look up at the city sky, I am overtaken by gratitude, by the weightlessness of hope fulfilled.

Probation

Graduation is Tuesday, and we have just found out what stations we each will be going to. The list is hotly anticipated, and everyone is sent to the place where the instructors think they would be best suited. As with everything in drill school, it's a competition, with the best of the class expecting to go to the best stations. I'm going to Rainier Valley, and I'm not sure why. The valley is known for being full of hardasses and rough-and-tumble crews. A few classmates are jealous that I got assigned to such an eminent position.

I'm flattered for a brief moment but then brace myself for the impact after the instructors say I'm in for it. They give me advice and say that the Rainier station likes to fire people, so I need to show up with my A game. Great, just when I jump over one hurdle, an even bigger one shows up. The instructors also say our best bet is to not tell our new crews anything personal about ourselves, to go full throttle on anything they tell us to do, and keep as low of a profile as possible.

After finding out that my new crew will be at drill school graduation, I'm immediately overcome with regret. I shouldn't have invited the guy I just started dating, Robert. They will know everything about me before I even show up to my first shift if I bring him. I can't put myself in that position, can't jeopardize my career for someone I've only seen a few times in the past few months. Rationally, I know what I need to do, but morally, ethically, spiritually, I know that what I'm about to do is wrong. I disinvite him.

Graduation isn't a great experience. I'm wracked with guilt, completely overwhelmed by it. I've fought so hard to be open in drill school, and here I am, willfully stepping back into the closet, this time hurting the guy I'm dating in the process. Graduation is painful both inside and out. As I internally regret my cowardice, I smile and shake hands with every instructor and classmate and high brass in the department. Only problem is, my right hand is still injured.

The stronger the handshake, the more accepting and congratulatory the person. It is a masculine expression of emotion, their way of showing they care, and fucking shit it hurts like hell. During every handshake, I tell myself not to show the pain in any way. I want them to know how grateful I am to be one of them. The pain drains my body of all energy. I hope they can't see the pain in my face; I try to show them the light in my eyes instead, the light of the dream come true. That light is bright, but the pain is saturating. I cannot feel my hand anymore. It's numb, except for the firm shake of victory.

The first day of operations, I'm confident in my ability to perform but petrified of the social implications of being an outsider. Someone once said that when a man walks into a room, his whole past walks in with him. I imagine that most of the people in my class are wracked with anxiety on their first day, but I'm not sure if many feel the absolute frenzy of fear that I'm walking into this department with. I've never been a nervous person, but I've become an utterly anxious man somehow, weighed down by the dreaded outcomes of my fears. I keep telling myself it will work out, it has so far, but I struggle to believe it.

In the moments before my first shift, I don't have time to keep thinking about this. I need to be present. Here. Now. No distractions.

Within minutes of taking my position on the truck, the engine officer pulls me into his office.

"Are you afraid?" His bloodshot eyes look straight into mine without hesitation. There is weaponlike precision in his glare.

"I was told to be, sir." The truth, my only response.

"You should be. We've fired recruits before. I don't know what this probationary firefighter title is all about, because you're a recruit to me. That's how it was when I came in, back when this department was actually tough."

"Yessir."

"What's wrong with your hand?" My hand is wrapped with an awkward amount of KT tape.

"Nothing, sir. I think I might have sprained it in drill school, but I've been working on it for weeks. It's almost healed." I'm surprised at the strength in my voice considering how weak I feel inside.

"Great, they sent us a gimp. What is this department coming to?" He sends me out of his office after some heated warnings about how he will be testing me and making me prove that I can hack it.

Within moments the bells hit. Screaming bells, straight to my bowels.

Heartbeat pounding in my eardrums, sweat beginning to drip, the engine rushes out of the station and we're off. It's a medic call. A Med 7, CPR in process. My first call on my first shift in my first minutes of being in operations, and I'm going to do CPR with an injured hand. Perfect.

"Rookie, get ready. You're going to do most of the compressions."

I've never done compressions before. They say it's a rite of passage, that it's worse than you think. It's all a haze until I'm hovering over this limp body, gloved hands together, left palm doing all the compression because my right hand feels like an exposed bone fragment again. I focus all my energy on my left palm, keeping my elbow locked, using my torso as the force that keeps blood pumping through this man's veins. A few of his ribs crack like dry twigs under the compressions. I do two minutes, switch out, have a two-minute break where I use a bag-valve mask to help him breathe, then switch out again and get more compressions. There's that old rhythm, *ah-ah-ah-ah, staying alive, staying alive.* The medic tells me to slow it down just a bit but that I'm doing great. I must be on my sixth round of compressions when they call it. He's not coming back. This was a long time coming. The family members surround us in the house. Wails of grief. I walk toward life outside, leaving the shrinking room behind.

"Good job, rookie," the lead medic says as she puts her hand on my shoulder. "Was that your first one?"

"Yes, ma'am," I say. My voice is sterile.

"They're never easy, but you'll get the hang of it. We get them back half the time. We're the best in the country." The calm empathy in her voice steadies me.

"You did the best compressions out of anyone," she says, her smile full. "They sure won't tell you that, but you did."

I try to form a smile as thanks, but she turns and races off to other people who need her.

"Not bad for a cold-blooded killer," my truck partner says, and laughs as we climb into the truck.

Within the hour we get a fire response. I bunk up and jump on the truck, putting my facepiece and SCBA cylinder on and listening to the report on the radio. It's a kitchen fire, with smoke billowing out of the two-story house.

When we pull up, fire is escaping from the eaves of the roof. This is what I've been waiting for these past three years. It's here, on my second call and first hour of shift, no less.

I'm told to throw a ladder, so I grab one and throw it in the exact way taught in drill school, which I find out is not what they want. Great. Another firefighter puts a ladder to the roof and we all climb up. I use a tool to pull back the roof that another firefighter is cutting with the chainsaw. The roof beneath my feet is soggy and covered with moss and feels like it's about to open up. I move toward the peak of the roof but see flame lapping out of the hole. Back over the soggy part and down to the base of the hole, I see someone lifting the firehose up to us, so I grab it and put out the flames. Soon the fire in the kitchen below us is out, and we have a large part of the kitchen roof removed, making sure the fire didn't extend past that area.

It takes a while to clean up. We nail tarps to the roof so that there is still some shelter in the house, then go inside and clean out all the charred insulation from the walls and the burnt wood. It's a mess of black syrup that sticks to everything, and it's hard work to clean out all the damage in the kitchen and the bathroom. After a few hours, we've done enough and are back in service for calls.

"Damn, rookie, first CPR and first fire all before lunch. You're a black cloud." The term is a nickname for people who seem to attract crisis. You don't want to be a white cloud, not in this profession.

The day continues in the same pattern. A dock comes loose during a storm on Lake Washington and starts thrashing into an expensive boat next door. My hand, violently angry with the use demanded of it, holds the dock in place with the pike pole that I use to keep it from hitting the boat. After some time, with severe pain in my hand, we manage to tie the dock off and pull it to the safety of the shore.

"I didn't think I'd be doing more work on the water," I say to the crew.

"We have to be jack-of-all-trades in this line of work," my officer speaks into the headsets as we drive away.

"Speaking of jack-of-all-trades, I hear you were in the Navy and you're a writer," my partner in the back says.

I don't know what to say. There is a short silence.

My officer cuts back in and laughs. "What, you didn't think we'd google you before you showed up?" he says. "Sounds like you've had quite the life so far, Mr. Author."

They know already. Panic sets in, but they continue to talk as if the information changes nothing and they aren't too interested. They ask about the Navy a little, what my job was, and I find out my tailboard partner was in the Navy as well. We tell a few sea stories.

The mood from the start of the day and the intensity of being a newcomer has now shifted, and I feel a little bit like a part of the crew after having fought alongside them so much already. I like them. They're a bunch of good guys. I feel accepted.

I think of Robert and how I could have brought him to graduation anyway. It wouldn't have changed anything. That was my cowardice. But then there's that flag of mine, the book I put out into the world at my most courageous time, and it keeps doing all the work for me. It may not have been a commercial success, but it continues to inspire me and push me forward. It is a personal success and has given me this moment of being openly gay on my first day on the job, even when I am too fearful to use my voice. That younger, more virile version of me is still speaking into the world, still proclaiming his truth when I cannot find my tongue. I am thankful for that young man I was before, for breathing courage back into my bones.

There are many calls that day, and I don't sleep much that night. When I leave the station in the morning, I feel the high of having just finished a race, the elation of accomplishment, the joy in doing. As I drive down Rainier Avenue, a part of town I seldom inhabit, I'm thankful to be done with the first day on the job. I got my first CPR, and hot damn I finally got my first fire!

I had scheduled an MRI after the big first shift today, as I had promised the doctor that night in drill school. After the MRI, the doc tells me he will call with results in a few hours. I make my way back to the boat, relieved and exhausted. Winter on the boat again. This is my third winter and, man, it's always colder than I remember. I take a nap after turning on all my space heaters.

The phone rings to wake me up. It's the doctor. He's fervid.

"You need surgery immediately if you don't want to be permanently disabled. There's such little blood flow to the scaphoid bone that even a fracture can cause it to die, and you have a full break. You shouldn't have been working."

Three weeks after the accident, I find out the full extent of my injuries. I had worked for three weeks with a broken bone in my hand. Three weeks of sacrificial bone.

Surgery is scheduled for the week before my thirtieth birthday, to implant an inch-long screw through the scaphoid bone of my right hand. I am awake through the entire procedure and watch the screw as it is drilled into my hand on the X-ray monitor. They put a sheet between the procedure and me so that I can't see, and the nurses are amused by my curiosity to watch the X-ray screen. I can feel, through the numbness of the drugs, the vibrating infiltration of the metal into my bone. The drugs make everything slightly funny. As I get up after the operation, the nurses ask if I need more painkillers. I laugh them off, but by the time I get to the car where my mom is waiting to drive me home, the itching pain in my hand begins to throb in waves of ascending severity. My mom takes me to the pharmacist, where we impatiently wait for the remedy. Thank heaven for my mother and her soothing care. Against her protestations, I say I'll stay on the boat by myself. I have to go back to work in a few days and need to get back into my rhythm. After many promises that I'll call if anything goes awry, I shuffle to my boat in the deepening winter and find that living on a sailboat with one hand proves even more challenging than I'd imagined. I've turned into a one-handed pirate aboard this *Blazin' Guns*, and instead of a hook I have a screw. Shiver me timbers. Shiver me freezing butt off.

Back at work they assign me to modified duty, where all the broken people go to mend their bodies while still attempting to do work. I'm embarrassed to go back to the training facility. To me it's a sort of failure. I'm not out there with my fellow recruits proving that I'm capable. In my bashful state, I show up to work alongside the same instructors that had just trained me in drill school. My new tasks will be to ready the training facility for the next round of recruits. To my great surprise, instead of making me feel like a failure, the instructors are impressed by my ability to overcome pain and finish drill school with a broken bone. Even the chief makes sure I know how impressed he is that I had the grit to finish.

"You did chainsaw appreciation with a broken hand! And finals week?" the chief says, with a creased look of shock on his face and a nod of approval.

"Even got his first fire in ops before he found out," another instructor makes sure to note.

"That's some old school shit right there," another instructor adds. "That's how it used to be, before we got all soft."

It's apparent that I've passed some sort of test, and in some way they look at me not as a recruit anymore but as a comrade. A bit of the stress is taken off me, but I still don't want to be here. I want to be out in the field, so I focus all my attention on physical therapy and getting myself healed up, which the doctor warns might be a while because I waited so long to get surgery.

I make a trip back to my station in Rainier Valley and tell them everything that's happened. They are less impressed than the drill instructors, but they are eager to keep me in the loop and train me so I don't fall behind. We come up with a plan where I can keep getting all my nonphysical tests done and gain experience. They invite me to come back to the station while I heal, to be part of the team, and to keep working. I'm thankful for their openness and spend my time going back and forth between the training facility and the fire station, performing double duty.

Throughout the rest of the nine-month probationary period, recruits are tested on a daily basis with drills, paper tests, and EMS and fire calls, and they are mandated to prove their ability. Failure to do so will cost us a job. We must pass every test or risk falling behind. Like drill school, a retest is allowed once or maybe twice, but a retest at all is considered bad form, and you don't want that sort of attention on you. I know that I am under the microscope, for my broken hand and for being gay, so I do my best to stay hypervigilant and motivated, showing no signs of weakness and every sign of aggression.

My hand heals up in six weeks. The doctor is wildly impressed and doesn't quite believe it. He makes me prove to him that I'm healed by doing physical therapy at the highest level, in front of him and the nursing staff, all these pulleys and weights and flexion exercises. The room gets stuffy from my sweat. The nurses make a sort of game of it.

The doctor says that I will be even stronger than I was before because of the metal in my bone. I find a bit of comfort there, seeing all my past injuries as stronger places in my body, my mind, and my spirit, like some living form of *kintsugi*, the Japanese art of repairing broken things with gold lining.

I am released back to operations and have a huge deadline: I have one month to prove that I can do every one of my truck skills before I am sent to the next point of training. Otherwise, they could make me redo all the truck work and I would have to graduate with the next class. I will not let that happen.

Every day I show up to work ready to throw ladders, use chainsaws, prove that I can operate all the power tools and equipment, understand the entire inventory on the truck and the engine, then take all these skills and put them into action. I am unrelenting, even as the bloodshot eyes of the engine officer hover over me, and he blows cigar smoke into my face as I conduct the drills, even as I compete with my senior tailboard partners and beat one of them at confined space self-extrication. There is a finish line ahead of me, and in order to catch up to my class I must reach it. I push, focused and determined, and the final test comes.

I make it through the final day of the three-month truck training process. The truck crew recommends that I pass their portion of probation. Somehow, in the first three months in operations, I've overcome every challenge that had been put in my path, worked double-time, overcome the broken bone and healed it, and passed every test I needed to, even as an openly gay man. I'm moving on. I'm back in the pack.

The next station I am sent to is in Madison Park for the fire engine portion of probation. It's a stark contrast to my experience in the department so far. The district is a quiet one and the number of calls I go on plummets, so I spend my days working on gear, reading and studying my homework, drilling, and going on the occasional call. I'm disappointed that they sent me to a slower station, after having a riot of an experience in the Rainier Valley. I go a little stir-crazy with the sudden change.

Then one day I get a fire call.

The emergency lights flash on and the sirens blare. We speed to Capitol Hill, past so many places where my memories reside. I'm putting my SCBA air bottle on as we see a great pillar of smoke from blocks away. All my gear is in place as we pull up to a two-story house that looks like a giant chimney.

"Wye bundle to the front door," my officer bellows, so I jump out of the engine and grab a huge stack of hose, then run to the first engine. My partner connects it and I flake the hose out toward the house.

At the front door the smoke fills my lungs as I inhale a breath that feels like death. I drop to my knees and call for water as I put the facepiece on and connect to the cylinder on my back. Sweet air. When water fills my hose, I rush into the billowing house and go blind. Thick smoke and heat. I wipe the condensation from my facepiece with my glove and get slightly better vision. The hose from the first engine is on the floor in front of me, and my facepiece goes black again. Feeling the first hose with one hand, I use it as a guide as I pull my hose in with my other hand. I stumble through the living room and over a lump. Someone says to be careful; there's a body in the room. Through the darkness I find an orange flicker of light in the back room. As I get closer, there is a sound of rushing and tearing, the sound of destruction. The fire on the ceiling comes into full view. It looks alive, moves across the ceiling like a monstrous serpent. The first-in engine company is flowing water on the beast. I open my nozzle and help them finish it off. Soon the room crackles and spits. The sounds of simmering, then all is quiet for a brief moment.

The clamor of windows being opened, of chainsaws on the roof, of searches being conducted in the rooms upstairs come together violently as the smoke recedes and the house is ripped open to the daylight.

On the living room floor lie the charred remains of the one we couldn't save. The family is outside, crying, trying to come in.

"We tried to save her, but we couldn't get her out." The family's wails echo through the house. I can't take my eyes away from the body, charred like the victim of a volcanic event. Someone places a blanket over a form that looks anything but human. The fire has claimed her.

Somebody pushes me out of the way, and someone else tells me to go upstairs and look for hot spots. As the truck teams pull the walls open to reveal amber embers, I drench the walls with foam from my hose. The walls of the house are black. The belongings, the furniture and clothes, all are charred with death and soaked, creating a pungent liquid that covers our gear.

My air bottle's low-air alarm sounds, so I walk out into the sunny day. Reporters show up with cameras searching for the story. The bystanders are effusive in their emotional need to convey what happened. The firefighters take turns, some rushing in, others like myself remove their soiled gear and drink copious amounts of cold water. Fire engines and trucks line the streets from all directions. Lights flash. Radios herald commands. I see a few familiar faces from Rainier Valley and say hi. The sun is vibrant and the sky is blue. The birds haven't stopped singing, even for us.

Neighbors are showing up, begging for information.

"Is everyone okay?"

I don't know how to respond. I tell them I don't know.

In the chaos I find a spot away from all the attention and sit on the tailboard of the fourth-in engine. I lean back, drenched in sweat and ash. I can't shake the image of her. She was ninety years old, maybe older. A grandmother, loved. I am humbled by my role in all this. As the bustling scene around me continues its frenzied motions, my mind absorbs the true extent of what I've signed up for. This is what I've fought so hard for, the ability to rush into these places, to fight for others.

I awake in the middle of deep sleep to the horrendous shrieks of alarm bells. It's game time. As I put my pants on and race to the engine, I do my best to wake up and remind myself where I am and what I need to do. After I put my bunker pants and coat on, I jump into the engine as we flare out of the station in a blur of light and noise. On the ride there I force myself to wake up fully, to gather all my wits so that I can do my job. Shaking off the drunkenness of deep sleep and sobering up to be completely present for the job are sometimes a difficulty. The haze clings to me.

We make it to a homeless shelter downtown. There is a gas leak. We must evacuate everyone immediately. No questions. Get them out now. As I climb the stairs up to the second floor, I walk into a scene I have never seen before. Hundreds of homeless people line the long halls of a huge room full of cots, spilling out of the additional bunk rooms where crowds of them sleep. I walk through and tell them all to exit the building; it's not safe to be here. They try to gather their things, large garbage bags bursting with possessions. I tell them to leave everything. There is no time. Their reluctance to leave their few remaining things reveals more than I wish to witness. This crowded place, with its dirty floors and stench of body fluids, is all they have left.

I'm transported back to the South Pacific. A ship is sinking. It is full of people desperately in search of a better life and doing anything in their power to get to the United States. As part of my ship's deployment, and as a part of the VBSS (visit, board, search, and seizure) team, I am in the unique position of assisting these people. As we load the small rigid-hull inflatable boat with as many passengers as we can hold, I can't help but look at the plethora of faces that overflow from the sinking fishing vessel. Their expressions are pained and fearful, hungry. As they hold their children, they assist the elderly to stand on the rocking vessel. My small boat taxis between sinking boat to Navy frigate, back and forth, until all the refugees are on the steel decks of the warship.

A small tent city is set up on the highest deck of the ship, the only space large enough to fit the crowd of people. We feed them, give them blankets, and do our best to make them feel comfortable, but there is little protection from the elements. When the winds howl and the rains drive hard enough, we huddle them into the helo hanger until the storm passes. When the night clears, people pass out under their tents, sleeping on mats the sailors have used for workouts throughout the deployment.

I stand guard over the group of refugees, and the ship voyages back toward land to return them to the country they have run away from. There is no other option. The noise of their sleep, small children's moans and old men's snores, filters through the night. There are many stars visible. Too many. A plentitude of stars that makes me feel mortal, exposed. The fragility of life and the pulsating enormity of the universe, expounded by the endless expanse of sea, fill me with nausea. I hold my gun for comfort. Steady steel. I can't help feeling connected to these sleeping people. What terror could cause them to fill an old boat to the tipping point and set out to sea? What motivation could drive them to such risk? The night sky looms over us. The darkened sea swallows the light.

After days of travel, we make it to Guatemala and begin unloading the refugees. There is gratitude in their faces, thankful to have survived the terrible journey, to be rescued by us. They thank me, one by one, as they pass before me on their way to new struggles. In their faces I see trepidation, the unknown future that awaits them upon their return home. This is a somber walk toward destiny. Have we rescued them? Have we condemned them? Both?

Their transitory faces merge with the faces of the homeless as I march them out of their shelter in downtown Seattle. I feel as if I am repeating something, a déjà vu, a purgatory. I have signed up for the job of helping, of assisting, and here I find myself in the fluctuations of the unknown. What has become of those refugees now?

More than five hundred people are evacuated out of the shelter, five hundred people on the streets of Seattle in the small green space across the street in the depth of dark morning. After the building is safely cleared, the gas leak is found and the energy crews begin to rectify the situation.

The five hundred people stand in huddles outside, keeping themselves warm in the chill morning. They ask me when they can go back inside. They need their clothes to get to their jobs on time. They can't miss work.

For whatever reason, I am less focused on the immediate help we are giving these people than on the long-term assistance they need in order to better their lives. I feel compelled to help them solve their problems somehow. There is a great drive in me to be with them on their entire journey, a journey I hope may see better days in the future. My religious upbringing flashes before my eyes, the missionary's slideshows of helping people in remote villages. In those villagers' faces I now see the refugees, in the refugees' faces I see the homeless, in the homeless, I now understand, I see myself. Across the decades of my life, from child to young man to adult, I realize that I have been created, conditioned, encouraged to be this in role, and in that actualization, I've come full circle. I have no idea if I can make a difference at all, much less effect a positive change in anyone's course, but what I can do is be here for these people right now, in the haze of morning exhaustion, in the terror of midnight danger; be here to help bring calm and assistance to a dangerous place. All around me are faces of people like me, fighting their pasts, caught in the tides of history, fighting and losing battles that have landed them in this place. All around me, people trying to find freedom from the bondage of their past and present, trying to find a better future.

When the leak is fixed, we guide the crowds back into the shelter. They thank me for my work, but I don't feel comfortable taking thanks for doing my job. I'm just profoundly grateful for the honor of having this work.

The rumors find their way to me, first small and seemingly inconsequential. People want to know about my writing. How much of it is true. Is it antigovernment? Rumors continue to mount. I have a new partner every day on my shift, so I get to meet people from the other stations and battalions. The rumors grow in boldness.

One day my new partner, whom I haven't met or even said a word to yet, walks up to me and says, "I know you're gay."

I pause, unsure of my next move. The only thing to do is extend my hand. "I'm Lance," I say.

He introduces himself, a prior Army Ranger, but presses me for an answer to his statement. I nonchalantly give it to him. He asks about the mayor, my military history, Don't Ask, Don't Tell. He tells me we're brothers, but something doesn't feel right.

My exposure comes with great misgivings. Should I be this honest? Will someone fire me? I do my best to be genuine and honest, but this is strange territory, and it's obvious that the department is in the same boat that I am. I've asked around, and while people speculate that there could be a few gay guys in the department, there are clearly no men who are open about it. No one really knows how this will go. In a few years I'll eventually meet another gay fireman, a Marine Corps veteran who is married with three kids, but he is a guarded man and keeps that information private, which I view as him protecting his family. I would probably do the same thing if I had kids right now. It will be another five years before another openly gay guy will serve as a firefighter with me, and I will have the honor of assisting him on his path to get hired.

Soon there are rumors circulating that I am turning people in for their bigotry and racism. People say I'm telling the mayor everything I see, like I'm some sort of spy. The rumors change every time I hear them, but they are spoken boldly. Every time I have the opportunity, I ask where they heard the rumor. What exactly was it? Who was the source? In a time when I should be working on my probationary checkoffs and tests, I'm worried about what people are saying about me and how I can fix it.

I tell myself I don't need to give any credence to the rumors; give them no attention and they'll go away. But they don't. They continue, and change, and morph, and keep coming back to me like some sort of test from my probationary trials. I still don't know what the real story is.

The rumors seem to come from my last station in Rainier Valley, a reality that cuts deep to my core. It can't be the guys I worked with. I don't believe it. Again and again, however, I hear the rumors, so I try to figure out how I can confront the gossip. Someone in the valley needs their shift covered, so I volunteer to go back into the lion's den and face it.

Within minutes of being there, I'm confronted by a crew from a different shift. It feels as if the lions are circling; they could attack and rip me apart if they desired. A few are talking to me directly, but I see the others standing back, listening, lying in wait.

My confronters bark at me. "Did you do it?"

With equal force, I say, "I have no idea what you're talking about, and everyone has been telling me about it. I'm an honest guy, so honest that I always get into trouble for it. If I had a problem with someone, I would tell them directly. I wouldn't talk about them behind their back or turn them in." I'm heated. The blood fills my face.

A guy from a different crew walks up to us and says, "What are you guys doing, trying to stir up trouble? Talk about this some other time."

As the day goes on, we lightly continue the conversation, and it becomes clear to me that my crew had nothing to do with the rumors. I realize that wherever the rumor originated, it came from a root of fear, and somehow people were afraid of me. I'm not sure if my aggression at facing the rumor works, but it does feel as if it lightens some of the tension in the firehouse. It seems the rumors are a test. I think I pass, even though no one says anything straight out. The fact that I'm here, right now, is my answer.

After that shift, the rumors mostly die away. Another obstacle passed. Another challenge overcome. But there are still months left to go.

Pride

Spring turns to summer. It's a beautiful day to return to the training compound to do quarterly training with my crew. I've been driving the engine a little every day to gain experience behind the wheel. After probation is over, I'll be expected to do all the duties of a firefighter. Being a driver is one of those tasks, and probably the most intimidating. It comes with a great amount of responsibility: the firefighters in the building rely on the driver to get water through the hoses to fight fires. As I drive into the training compound and see the burn building and high tower we drilled in for months, I'm transported back to drill school, the yelling instructors, the engine and truck drills, the pain.

I pull the engine up and park it by the classroom building. Today we're doing race and social justice training, a city program meant to educate people on diversity and its challenges and successes. We talk about implicit bias and institutional racism. We're asked to share stories at the end, and I get to hear about how difficult it was for other minorities throughout the fire department's history. People who have been in the department for twenty years share their stories. I wish I could say it's shocking to hear of the prejudice they experienced on their journeys, but I've seen enough myself to understand. The city and the fire community are doing their best to address the issues to make our city a better place for all. It's hard work and causes the room to fill with tension and emotion. Deep inside me I fall more in love with my city. Here, I don't feel like the only one who is working for change. Here, I don't feel alone. While my road has had its own sets of difficulties, training like this, and a department that listens, is more than I have ever known.

But the process is arduous. I hear of the most blatant forms of discrimination, prejudice, and outright hatred in these people's experiences. While these outright biases have been abolished, the subtleties and subtext persist. These histories inform our present, and it is difficult to wrestle with them.

It's clear to me that there are minorities to this day in my department who have major obstacles to overcome, myself perhaps included. The most obvious and much talked-about example being women, who make up less that 10 percent of the department. There are a few women in the room today, and their stories and the things they've had to deal with truly sadden me. It astonishes me that they are so willing to be open. I feel weak in comparison. Although most people know that I am gay, I've barely given myself a voice to respond to anything. I feel silent, in many ways. Unlike these strong women. They speak their truth. They have fought for decades to be here. How am I the first openly gay guy here? There have been lesbians working in the department for decades, and they've had it much harder. Being a lesbian woman in a straight, white, male-dominant profession... I'm completely inspired by the courage of these firefighters, filled with deep respect and gratitude toward them, their struggle, their hard work and dedication. Thank God for them. Beautiful, wonderful people.

After training, I see an instructor from drill school. My first thought brings me back to him screaming in my face, calling me a liar, making my life hell. I swallow the memory, choke it down, and greet him with a gregarious handshake.

"Lance, nice to see you. Can I talk with you for a minute?

He pulls me into an empty classroom and goes straight to work.

"First off, if I am out of line in any way, you just tell me to shut up." His rehearsed statement throws me off-balance. Tell him to shut up, yeah, right before getting punched in the face. He is no less intimidating than he was in drill school. A beast of a man.

"I've heard some rumors. Normally I don't give them any thought, but you're one of my recruits, and I want to make sure I do something about it. Your reputation is on the line."

I immediately know what he's talking about. Here I am again, back to the accusation of being dishonest, accused in drill school and accused in probation. I thought the rumors were over. My skin is covered in red blooms of anxiety. I can't see them, but I can feel their heat.

He talks in vague terms, uncharacteristic of him. I know this topic is a sensitive one. He dances around, waiting for me to acknowledge the real topic. He talks about the rumors, but he doesn't bring them to a conclusion. I take the bait.

"They aren't true, sir, and I went there to face those rumors head-on. The truth is, I think the root of these rumors is about something else entirely, because I usually get in trouble for being too honest."

He stops to think about my response as I think about the training I just came out of. I can't walk down the hall after social justice training before I'm faced with another obstacle. But I'm empowered by those who have come before me and face up to my part.

"So *that* is true, then?"

I breathe in deeply. "Yes. I get it," I say. "I'm the first one. It's going to take some time for people to get used to that idea. I was in the Navy during Don't Ask, Don't Tell. I get it."

Just like when he accused me of lying in drill school and I bared my honesty to him, his voices changes, softens to a tone of understanding. "But discrimination is illegal here."

I don't say anything, shocked by the reality that I'm safe now and that he stands behind that safety. Such a foreign feeling: to trust that I'm in a rightful place.

His voice is full of conviction. "That doesn't mean it won't be difficult. Women have had a rough go at it, and it's still difficult for them. My girlfriend works for a different department, and she had to sleep on a mat in the gym because she couldn't share the communal bunk rooms with the men—their wives wouldn't let her. Things change, but it takes a lot of work."

"I've been trying my best to just let it go, sir. To just show up, and to do my job, because that is what we're all here for."

He looks at me, and his face goes back to its normal confidence. He stands up a little straighter and I follow suit, as if we shift the burden on our backs to a more comfortable position.

"Then get out there, Garland, and go do work."

I do, and as I drive the fire engine back to the station, I'm somehow stronger from that instructor's acceptance.

It's June. I have three months before probation is over, before I am a legitimate firefighter. No recruit is safe. We could still get fired, although we'd have to do something really bad at this point, but there is still a high bar for us to prove ourselves worthy of the job. The past nine months have been difficult, but we've risen to the occasion. We get a little street cred for that, and are treated better because of it.

I occasionally get to work with one of those strong women from training, a respected lieutenant with more than twenty years of experience. She's married to a wonderful woman, a retired San Francisco firefighter, and has a few kids. They've lived openly for decades. My colleague has the humbleness of a true champion, and I won't learn from her that she's a prior Olympian who played handball in the 1984 and 1988 games and won gold medals in the Pan American Games and U.S. Olympic Festival.

She asks me one day, almost nonchalantly, if I would walk in the Pride Parade.

"We have a lot to celebrate this year," she says, referring to the fact that the Supreme Court is about to rule on marriage equality and it's looking very likely that they will make it the law of the land. Everyone is teeming with excitement about it. Seattle is ablaze with chatter.

I smile at her, the light in her eyes reflected by mine. A moment of uncertainty from me dampens my smile. I say, "But do you think it's a good idea?"

She responds with kindness. "It is. You deserve it."

With that she walks away, making it no longer an issue. It is simple, an invitation to a parade. My own strength is dwarfed by hers. Over the next few days I am riddled by doubt. Marching in the parade as a probationary firefighter has huge implications. The media will be there, and high brass of the department will see who attends. In essence this will be a huge public coming-out for me. Do I have the strength for that? Nightmarish possibilities come into my head. What if someone in the department takes offense? What if that starts an internal investigation like it did for me in the Navy? What if that pisses someone off and they make it their mission to get me fired? I'm not safe yet. I don't have a job, officially. Everything is still on the line. I have no right to be so overly confident, so flamboyant, so gay.

I fall back into fear, remembering how I told Robert he couldn't come to drill school graduation. Shame fills me like I'm a sinking ship. Who do I think I am? I'm just a man who has no power and is unable to bring his boyfriend to a celebration, a right most people wouldn't even acknowledge. If I can't even muster the courage to risk taking him to a ceremony, how on earth could I muster the courage to walk through Seattle as an openly gay firefighter?

After I'm diminished by my fear and wallow in it for too long, the darkness dissipates. I start to see a new perspective. Her words, "You deserve this," echo in my mind. I imagine the beauty of walking in the parade in uniform, the first time I've ever walked in the parade. That little daydream fills me with happiness.

I think back to all the people in that training, how hard it's been for them, and how they continue to show up for the job. I think about how hard it was for me to get this job, the years of work, the years of fighting for my rights, the years under the iron fist of Don't Ask, Don't Tell and my childhood—years of silence. Here is this grand opportunity to take a stand, to give myself a voice, to fully and completely be myself with pride and gratitude, with a huge group of people who have fought for me to do that very thing.

I grow stronger in the knowledge that a community of people surrounds and supports me. After all, it isn't just me standing here in this uniform today; it's whole tides of people who have fought for their rights, and in so doing have fought for our rights, for me to have the opportunity to even consider this idea.

That is why I choose to march in the parade.

I'll face my fear to walk in the parade as a probationary firefighter.

It's June 27, 2015, the day after the Supreme Court's decision to make marriage equality a federally recognized right. I'm at the fire station on duty, and everyone is abuzz with the historic news. Even if I were too scared to march in the parade tomorrow, there's no getting away from the current of this profound moment. Social media has turned rainbow-colored, and an outpouring of support and cheers comes from every angle. I receive text messages and emails, phone calls and social media posts congratulating me on this incredible moment, for all the hard work my little part in it required. People are so connected to this decision, so emotionally involved in marriage equality passing, that I feel as if I'm being embraced by society as a whole. Unfathomable just a few years ago.

During the workday I'm tasked with decorating the engine for the parade. Some wild force of fate has put the one engine reserved for the parade at my station. It's almost as if this moment is being handed to me on a platter. I'm told to use the unit markers we number our engines with, like Engine 30 or Engine 34, and instead to put PRIDE in all caps and rainbow colors as the marker. It's a twelve-by-ten-inch placard that I try to hand-draw with markers, which looks amateurish, so I create a document on the computer and have a local print shop laminate copies of it. I pick them up in the morning after I get off work, in a fresh new uniform, ready for the day's festivities.

When I get to Robert's house, he looks hesitant.

"You ready, babe?" I give him a hug and pull back to look him in the eye.

"Are you sure? I was thinking that maybe you should just go. This is your show." He looks sheepish, perhaps a little worried.

My heart races. I'm already afraid to show up in uniform and walk by one of the downtown stations during the parade. Will they reject me? Now he might ditch me. I don't want to do this alone.

Then I remember how I disinvited him to graduation. I'm the reason for his trepidations. I will not succumb to fear, not today.

"If you don't want to go, I completely understand. But I'd be honored if you'd walk with me."

He looks at me with a face full of relief.

We make our way downtown, and the city is wonderfully electric. It's like we just won the Super Bowl again, but this time it's a celebration of vivid colors and people of all different walks of life wearing the uniform of love. People wave and smile at me in my uniform. Robert walks with me as we make our way to the fire department space in the long line of parade floats. We are right by the mayor and the police. I think of Brock but don't see him in their unit. The parade starts just as we arrive, greeted by a group of female firefighters and their kids. One of them, a medic, walks straight up to me and says, "Wait, are you telling me that you're an out and proud gay fireman in Seattle?"

"Yes." I smile and ponder for a moment. "I am."

"I've waited twenty years for someone like you to show up."

Her face full of acceptance and encouragement fills me, enables my chest to swell, filling my lungs like full sails, my spine as straight as my sailboat's mast. Today I sail free.

I hand the PRIDE placards to a fellow firefighter, and she puts them on the engine as I grab a firefighter shirt for Robert. I introduce him to some of my coworkers, and they introduce me to their kids. The head of human resources, although he's not a firefighter, is truly the first openly gay man in the department. He greets us with hugs and thanks for showing up. He's done so much good work for me to be able to be here today, years of dedication, of breaking down walls. I thank him for everything.

And with that the engine starts rolling and the Seattle Pride Parade begins.

Robert and I have handfuls of stickers that we hand out to the kids lining the streets. People are cheering. Sheer jubilation reverberates through the echoing city. Color, vibrant and joyful colors, at every angle. We run this way and that, smiling and laughing and greeting the tens of thousands of people who stand in crowds like fields of wildflowers on the sidewalks, spilling out in happiness onto the street. Music blares from megaphones and huge speakers. It is the first time in my life that I feel like I'm in a music video, a larger-than-life production. I'm intoxicated by this celebration, by the cheers of the crowd, the love they exude and lavish on me. So many smiling faces, many from people whom I met on this long journey here, from the marriage-equality campaign. They call out to me, "Lance! Lance!" And I run to them and thank them and squeeze them in joy.

Soon the parade makes its way to the front of the Belltown fire station. The station crew are all sitting out in lawn chairs watching the festivities. Immediately I'm awoken from my reverie. Fear crawls up my calves and up my back to my neck. What will they think? I'll volunteer to be assigned to this station next year, and when I get there, old-timers will make snide comments about me being the crazy man screaming in the street during this parade.

But today, out of nowhere, someone comes up behind me and picks me up. When he puts me down, I turn around to a man dressed in a salmon-colored seersucker suit and hat, with a huge Jack Nicholson grin. He's from my current fire station on another shift.

"I'm proud of you, Lance," he says. He gives me another huge bear hug and lifts me off the ground before running off into the crowd.

The sails, full again. Mast straight.

Robert runs up to me and gives me a rainbow flag on a stick. His face, his whole being, is saturated with encouragement. He pushes me forward to the front of the fire engine. I lift that flag high overhead as the crowd cheers. Here I am, perfectly exposed, and blissfully rewarded for it. How on earth did this happen? It certainly wasn't because of anything I've ever done. This is a gift, the culmination of all these people's hard work, their sacrifices, their love. In this moment I lose myself completely, waving the flag high overhead, giving back all this joy to the crowds, thankful for being given this incredible reality. The darkness that I came from now fades away. This magnificent lightness of being.

I wave the flag high overhead, filled to bursting, water in my eyes evaporating from the utter bliss of it all, and raise my voice in a roar to the heavens, cheering as one with the crowd, celebrating our love.

I feel reborn—an emergence from cocoon to flight.

Probation draws to a close. I finish on time, even though my broken hand was a major obstacle, and whether it was a real obstacle or not, being the first openly gay man sure felt like an Everest of its own, even more than drill school and probation combined, at least in my head.

I've lived long enough to know that I have a long journey ahead. Graduating from probation is not the end; it's just a launching point of a new voyage. I have a whole career ahead of me, and there will be challenges that I certainly can't foresee. I wonder if those challenges will include being gay. My experience says it will. Life and all its intricacies didn't change completely with the Supreme Court's decision on marriage equality, and it certainly doesn't change just because one single dude shows up and does something that hasn't been done before. From this point on, I'm sailing in unknown waters, improvising as I go, and hoping that the winds will be in my favor. Who knows what storms we may face as we sail toward and beyond our dreams? What lands lie beyond the boundaries of my understanding? The great explorer Thor Heyerdahl once said, "Borders? I have never seen one. But I have heard they exist in the minds of some people." Maybe the great boundary of being the first openly gay man in the Seattle Fire Department wasn't really a boundary at all. Maybe that boundary was ingrained in me, a by-product of my time in the Navy, a learned response from childhood. Maybe, instead of being the first gay man in the department, the real victory is being able to stand here today courageous enough to be myself. Perhaps the victory is finally loving myself enough to give myself what I need, and in so doing, finding the ability to love others more completely.

Graduation at city hall. All the high brass, the chiefs of the department, all the drill school instructors, and even the mayor attend our momentous occasion. It's a haze of glory for us, twenty-six recruits graduating in alphabetical order, dressed in perfectly pressed, new uniforms. For the first time, we wear a black wool suit, white shirt, and black tie, and the finest and sharpest hat you've ever seen. We put our shields on our hat before we make our way out to the auditorium. It's like high school graduation. It's like college graduation, but it's more. It's like graduation from dreams to reality.

My name is called. My family—my wonderful family, the ones who persevered and made it here together—make more noise than all the other families, hooting and hollering, and cheering me on. So many members of my extended family show up. They are so proud. They cheer as I walk up to the podium and shake hands, this time with a stronger right hand, without pain, with all the chiefs. They give me a certificate and a badge in a velvet box. When everyone has received their diplomas and badges, we stand and face the American flag. It is time to swear the firefighter oath. We do so, with one voice, with one passion, and become official firefighters.

After swearing the oath, the main instructor from drill school tells us we can choose someone to pin our brilliant new badges on our uniforms. I point to Robert, who is sitting in the middle of my whole family.

I walk out into the crowd with my fellow classmates, right up to him.

I hand him the velvet box and say, "Will you?"

He nods bashfully, full of joy, and pins me as my whole family cheers and tears up. When he's done pinning me, I lean into him and kiss him in front of the whole department.

I kiss him, like a free man.

Maybe such dreams really do come true. I hope the same for you.

Face the Flame

Seattle Fire Station 2 sits on the corner of Fourth and Battery. I've only been working downtown for a few months, since I got off probation. The station is full of tradition and operates at a frenetic pace. The exterior has large red doors framed by white brick. Inside the apparatus bay are two fire engines, two ambulances, and one enormous ladder truck, all deep red. The interior walls are also painted white with red trim, decorated with black-and-white pictures of former firefighters and their rigs from various time periods of horse-drawn pumpers and the first motorized buggies. There are two fire poles, side by side.

The morning starts in the kitchen, which we all call the beanery, where a pack of old-timers sits drinking their acidic coffee. To me, they're like a pack of boxers after fights. Years of trauma and bouts with PTSD have battered their bodies and their positivity. The mood is especially dreary this morning. The crew last night didn't get any sleep. They're anxious for us, the relieving crew, to end their twenty-four-hour shift. Local politics is the chosen whipping boy this morning; thankfully it's not me. Complaints and negativity reign.

The newer firefighters, younger people like myself, make our way up to the second-floor gym for a break from the negativity. Once out of the old-timers' earshot, jokes bubble up with relief.

Someone turns on some upbeat music, and we all vent a bit about salty old dogs.

My friend Williams, from Vashon and drill school, comes up to me and playfully says, "Did I tell you how all the guys were asking about you before you showed up?"

"What about?"

"They heard you're gay, and they were worried that they were going to say the wrong thing to you."

"The wrong thing." I laugh, slightly perplexed.

His head and shoulders lean back in his hearty laugh. "I told 'em you're not that kind of guy. You're not an activist or anything, just a normal dude. You can handle the jokes."

"Just like the Navy," I say, with a wry grin and a wink.

I do some stretches as the phone in my pocket vibrates. I open it to see an email from the *Seattle Times.* Striding out of the gym and into the bunk hall, my heartbeat speeds up. I find my room and sit at the small table. They want to publish my op-ed tomorrow, about the Pulse nightclub massacre and the importance for the gay community to be visible. They need me to verify my identity as a city employee. As my fingers hover over the screen, attempting to respond, I wonder if this is a good idea.

Before I get a chance to reply, the alarm bells go off. I run to the fire pole, jump on it with my legs and arms wrapped just right so no skin touches the brass, and slide down to the first floor. At the engine I jump into my bunking gear and onto the fire engine as it speeds away.

Sitting backward in the cab and battling motion sickness, I put the air pack onto my back and secure the straps. We arrive at the emergency, a dumpster fire. In a flash I grab my helmet, pull the pack and myself out of the seat, exit the engine, grab two hundred feet of firehose on my right shoulder, and flake the hose out so there are no kinks in it when the driver sends me water. I kneel down on the hose, put my facepiece on, and open the air cylinder as the fire coils out of the dumpster like a cobra ready to attack. I slay it.

Back at the station we clean our gear and get ready for the next call, whatever it may be. The intercom calls all firefighters into the beanery. When we get there a woman with a broad smile and the nervousness of a newcomer stands at the front of the table.

"Hi, everyone. I'm Jenny, the new public information officer. The new fire chief has asked me to stop by the station and ask for volunteers to walk in the Pride Parade this year."

A flashover of laughter in the room dampens to snickers.

"Good luck finding someone." More laughter.

"That's a tough first job for you to get, ma'am," someone says as they try to contain their laughter.

"I think the lesbians usually take care of that."

"Well, that's just the thing, the fire chief wants a more diverse crowd to march in the parade. He wants us to have a good representation of the department." Jenny seems to get smaller in the face of the large group of men.

"You won't catch me dead marching in that parade," an old-timer states.

"I don't even own a thong," someone says to eruptions of laughter.

"I'll do it," I say.

All eyes turn to me, the laughter silenced.

"I marched last year when I was on probation. I plan on doing it again."

Jenny cautiously smiles at me.

A few of the faces in the crew seem to soften in realization. "Oh, yeah, there's a . . . there's nothing wrong with marching in a parade."

The crowd dissipates now that Jenny has found what she came for. As the crews leave the beanery, I shake Jenny's hand and quietly say, "You'll get the hang of it."

There isn't much time for contemplation as the calls come in successive waves: Aid calls of anxiety attacks, drunkenness, and minor trauma; medic calls of overdoses and cardiac issues; and a few fire alarms. I barely get the chance to respond to the *Times*.

By evening we're all starving. Downtown we eat a lot of comfort food to combat the stress. Tonight is fire pasta, a shift favorite. In the middle of eating the spicy chicken sauce, we get another call.

On the bathroom floor of a department store, a body lies in a sticky swamp of its own blood. My partner freezes at the edge of the liquid, so I push ahead of him and kneel down to the patient. He stabbed his own throat. The jagged knife lies sinisterly in the corner. His neck looks like a mangled can of tomato juice, a fountain of it. My hands encircle his throat to try to stop the bleeding, but it's no use. I feel his heart pump life out with each pulse. His eyes are glassy and distant.

"Give me the Israeli dressing," I command as the edges of my voice fluctuate, attempting to focus. "Where are the medics?"

I wrap the dressing around the man's neck, but it's not enough, so my bloody hands are back around his throat, holding pressure as the pulses slow. I feel his life leaving his body through my fingertips. We backboard the patient, push the gurney out of the store, through crowds, and put the stretcher into the medic rig. I release his neck as the doors close and the rig speeds away.

Back at the station, evening time, the lights are dimmed. Some of the old-timers are smoking cigars with the apparatus doors open. They murmur about the violence we just witnessed. My lieutenant stops me on the way to change my soiled clothes and boots and says, "You caught the brunt of that call. You're going to need to talk about it. Fire culture used to think talking about trauma was a sign of weakness, but that's not good for our mental health."

I nod, still feeling the patient's throbbing pulse in my hands, and say, "Thanks, lieutenant."

In the morning, after a night of calls, I walk into the beanery and see the *Seattle Times* unopened on the table. I leave the kitchen without my coffee and go up to the gym. Some minutes later the intercom calls me back down. The paper sits open on the table with my op-ed in plain view. I almost know the words by heart:

> I ask myself why I have this fear of visibility. I go to great lengths to convince myself that my fear of being visible, of being openly myself, is an irrational fear, unfounded and illogical. I do my best to reinforce within myself the thought that being visible is no longer dangerous, is no longer deadly. When I wake up in the morning and walk out into a world that has historically hurt me for being gay, a world that has harmed and killed others like me for hundreds of years, I encourage myself to believe that things are different, that things have changed. I imagine that some of the victims of the Pulse massacre in Orlando have faced the same internal battles, doing the hard work day in and day out to be open, to face the world, despite fear and oppression. I imagine that those victims have been inspired by a country that only a year ago was celebrating a historic equal rights win: the right to marry.
>
> Last year during Pride we were celebrating marriage equality. This year we mourn the victims of a massacre. It is hard for me to process that.
>
> Things have gotten better. My humble life is living proof of that. From an antigay religious upbringing to Don't Ask, Don't Tell and its repeal, marriage equality, and working for a city that supports my people, I know that things have gotten better for some.
>
> But for the victims of the Pulse massacre things got worse. As I sit here mourning their loss, painfully reminded of all my fears,

I reexamine my visibility. All too often it's easier for me to coast, to pass, present myself as a straight-acting, masculine male. I have that privilege, and that privilege is a tool I employ often. It's true, it is still very dangerous to be openly gay in this world. Last night is proof. That is why I have my fear of visibility. That is why I often pass as straight.

What matters is visibility. What matters is faith in humanity. Being visible is like a trust-fall; when we put ourselves out there for everyone to see, we need the support of those who receive that visibility. At the Pulse, people who put their trust in the world to keep them safe were violently and senselessly killed. I don't know how I could have protected them, but I will be searching for ways to protect those who remain.

As for my invisibility, I realize that my silence and my passing have done little to help them. My moments of visibility have done some work to give support to those victims, just as their visibility continues to strengthen our community and our country, even in light of such tragedy. I thank them for their truth, for their strength. I mourn their loss and will take this sorrowful moment to reexamine my visibility, and to recommit myself to do the hard, daily work of standing up for what matters, giving voice to the voiceless, and having hard conversations about our differences. Last year I was the first openly gay fireman to march in the Pride Parade with Seattle Fire, and I did it in in celebration of marriage equality. This year I'll march in remembrance of the victims of the Pulse massacre.

All eyes in the beanery are on me. My body goes slick with anxiety.

"Looks like someone's famous."

"You're definitely the first gay dude to show up here."

"Well, maybe not the first. There are rumors of other fart sniffers—"

"Male fart sniffers." Laughter.

"But you're the first one to be open about it."

Ten years later I'll find out that I'm not the first to be open about it. Assistant Chief Susi Rosenthal was one of the first cadre of women hired into the department and worked openly from the beginning of her career in 1980 as one of the first out lesbians. She'll tell me a story that I wish I'd known from the early days of my career.

In the 1990s firefighter Wayne Gott told Rosenthal in confidence that he came out to his crew when he was diagnosed with AIDS, and as his health failed him, his crew not only stood by him in support, but they also protected him and kept the matter private. He was out to his crew but not to the department at large. Tragically, his career and his life were cut short when he died of the disease.

I'll go in search of information about Gott and won't find much. Rosenthal said that Gott was a great guy and thought that he had a partner but couldn't remember his name. I'll find the AIDS Memorial Pathway in the Capitol Hill Neighborhood of Seattle, and on it are these words: "*Gifts to the AMP: AIDS Memorial Pathway have been made in memory of:... Mike Burkhardt and Wayne Gott.*"

The fact that Rosenthal is the only firefighter to ever tell me their story reiterates to me how quickly our queer histories are erased. I want to find out more about this man, this quiet pioneer of my community, but maybe this is all I'll ever know. Somehow, to me, the light of their brief story is enough. It has to be.

"Why did you say you're 'straight-acting'? Are you pretending? Do we even know who you are?"

"I just mean that I can pass as a straight man. It would be a lot harder for me if I were feminine."

"You're damn right. We'd definitely give you shit if you acted like a girl."

Their comments illuminate the crux of my experience as a gay man in this department. For all my trepidations about being the first openly gay man, that fact was never that big of an issue, as long as I didn't veer away from acceptable masculinity. When I later ask Rosenthal what her experience was like as one of the first openly lesbian firefighters, she'll tell me, "It was a way bigger deal being a woman in the department than a lesbian." Throughout my experience, I've tried to dig in and understand why gay men haven't felt comfortable serving openly, and here in the beanery is my answer. Often, I've been put on the level of women. Here, that's a negative thing. The takeaway from this experience as an openly gay man in the department is that sexism is the challenge. People treat women as less than, and they lump me in with women until I prove otherwise. My journey has been easier because of my privilege as a tall, athletic, white man. But from my perspective, between the strict gender roles of masculine and feminine, I've seen the true double standard. Women are held to a higher bar, though that is rarely acknowledged, required to be stronger than the men in so many ways. Perhaps not always physically, but certainly emotionally, socially, spiritually. Women do more work in just showing up every day and working against these stereotypes. For that, and for so many more reasons, I am proud to be placed in league with female firefighters everywhere. The grit of the women who do this work astounds me. Now I see that the roots of homophobia are entwined with the deep sexism of this culture.

The bells go off and I turn to rush out the door.

"We're going to talk more about this, Garland. Don't think you can get out of this one."

I ride the lights and sirens through the city, on my way to the next crisis.

The department needs public information officers like Jenny, so I volunteer in my off time. It's a wild ride from the start, giving press interviews at high-profile incidents and hosting public events. At the local blood drive, I encourage everyone present to donate, and take pictures and videos to encourage the public to do the same. People ask me when I will donate blood that day. I explain that I'm not allowed to because I'm gay. My scars from Don't Ask, Don't Tell are mirrored by the FDA's ban on my blood. But at this point I don't feel the shame like I used to; I face the injustice openly.

A few months later I attend my yearly firefighter physical and have a blood draw. The phlebotomist says I have easy veins and should consider donating. The vials fill easily as I tell him the story of overseeing the drive where I couldn't donate. At the end of my story, he gets confused. With half of the vials left to fill, my blood stops flowing. My veins close up.

Leave a Trace

As the horizon reveals itself in shades of ocher and tangerine, my surroundings slowly come into focus. We've been climbing by the light of our headlamps for hours. Back home, my life has been rendered unrecognizable. I've felt in the dark and have been wanting to give up this climb for weeks. Only my childlike wonder moves my footsteps higher.

I can't see the summit, only the headlights of my rope team partners, who are for the most part strangers. Here with them on Mount Rainier, single, my life has drastically shifted. Never did I think that I'd be climbing a volcano with grief fueling my footsteps. I'm not that kind of guy. This was supposed to be a victory climb, a childhood dream come true. Now it just feels like a casualty of youth, what little is left.

My team lead is slow, and the pace makes it hard to stay warm. Is it the altitude that makes everything he says frustrate me? We're only at eleven thousand feet, with almost four thousand feet of nearly vertical terrain to go.

He stops abruptly, waits for us to gather. "I think it's time for a break," he says.

I've only barely begun to feel warm again from the last break. Slowly, and with great effort, he takes off his pack, opens it, removes his down jacket, puts it on, pulls out a tightly packed bag, unfurls it, pulls out an energy bar, peels it open, and begins to take his first bite. The rest of the team has already eaten their snack and gathered their things. Our fearless leader is only halfway through his bar. The third rope partner and I put our packs back on, hoping to encourage him to continue. He doesn't seem to notice. My teeth start hitting each other, frigid and angry. In laborious fashion, he begins his ritual in reverse, taking care to stow everything perfectly in his pack before picking his ice ax up and finally saying, "Are you guys ready to—"

"Yes," we both state emphatically, stepping forward.

I'm frustrated because the team in front of us is breaking away. I should be with them. The alpine wind is gaining momentum, so I zip up my hood. I'm frustrated by more than this climb. No matter how hard I labor, no matter the amount of my passion, I can't seem to grasp the elusive thing I seek. Back home, most of my colleagues are married and have children. My life is nowhere near where I thought it would be by this point. What's wrong with me?

In my culture, the ability to get married is a new concept, a right we're still learning to believe is possible. For the first year of our relationship, my lover, Robert, told me how much he longed to get married, to have kids. We even named our future children. Things were aligning perfectly, same needs, same desires. He even allowed me the space to be my adventurous self and was my emotional support as I attempted to become Seattle's only openly gay fireman. I was in awe of his love, and it seemed the lasting kind.

In Paris, his romanticized city, a city I had just walked in for the first time, I proposed to him on the Pont de Bir-Hakeim over the Seine, the Eiffel Tower so close one could almost reach out and touch it. The stuff of storybooks. With a hired photographer to snap the surprise moment, I asked Robert to marry me by reciting a bespoke poem for the occasion. In my hands a box, not big enough for a finger, big enough for a wrist. The designer watch was inscribed with *Prorsum*, Latin for "Forward," and with it I wrapped his wrist with the promise of my time. I had finally found the man I would get on one knee for.

He didn't give me an answer.

We smiled and played the gracious couple, as the photographer escorted us about the city of love in his small sedan, taking pictures in all the most iconic places to commemorate the day. At the Charles de Gaulle airport, Robert called his mother and sister and told them that I had proposed. For a brief moment in time, although he had not said the word, it seemed we were engaged.

But as we flew out of that city of romance, there was something in his hesitation that presaged things to come. I looked away, in hope, in constrained patience, in a blind reach toward my dreams.

Many great writers have a chosen city. To my mentors, Salter and Hemingway and Kerouac, Paris was that city. But Paris refused to requite me. It was where we traveled to next, the rugged city of Lisbon, that chose me. Lisbon held my face as I raced through its stone streets, searching desperately for the nepenthe to my sorrow. Portugal gave me that antidote. I was only there because, as a doctor, Robert traveled the world, attending conferences to teach and learn the newest life-saving techniques. Lisbon had never been on my radar. Here I was in that legendary city, almost by accident. Robert worked while I explored a city with a deep past. I ran on the banks of the Tagus River, yearning for something that sent so many of their original explorers to sea, a future, the possibilities of dreams.

Through the saline air I ran, a half-marathon of touring by running shoe, when I came upon a souvenir shop that called me into it. Sweaty and short of breath, I browsed the quiet shop.

A kind look from the attendant inspired familiarity, and soon she guided me to a showcase of the life of the artist Abel Grade, who attempts to use light and movement in his works to create living pictures. I was inspired by one of his painted tiles in particular, with a yellow funicular in a city-lit night. I assured the attendant I'd return to purchase the tile, and we walked out of the shop together.

On the wall outside was a memorial with what looked like the words of a poem on it. My eyes lingered. The woman, with those kind, gray eyes, asked if she could translate the Portuguese for me. My lips turned upward in affirmation.

"The poet is giving thanks. Fully thankful in being, which reaches thanks from the pain that he really feels," she said, placing a hand on the back of my arm. "Pessoa lived in the apartment above this studio during 1917," she said, and moved her hand to the bronze tile on the wall. "There is a bookstore where you could buy an English version."

A day later Robert and I explored the castles of Sintra. We met the artist Lanca Semedo on the descent from the colorful Pena Palace. I bought a painting of the Alfama in downtown Lisbon as he whispered, "Art depends on the viewer. It can be beautiful or tragic depending on the perspective." He said it almost under his breath, to no listener in particular.

Later I found the bookstore the shop attendant had recommended. I bought the book *Lisbon Poets*, which included Pessoa's "Autopsychography." The translator had a much different view of the poem's meaning than the attendant did. Instead of the word "thankful," the defining word of the poem seemed to be "pretender."

Was I being thankful for what I was experiencing, even after a proposal without a yes, or was I simply pretending?

On my solitary rambling, through the city that gave my heart solace, I decided that my interpretation of the poem, of life, was like the merchant woman's. It was not my method to pretend. I would be wholeheartedly myself, and I would be thankful for anything that I received, anything that continued.

It was only later on that journey, on Portugal's golden beaches, that Robert said it was a maybe. In the Algarve we found a way to love beyond our expectations, and it was there that our relationship peaked in the Atlantic sunbeams, salt, and brown-sugar sand.

We spent two years postulating after that and continued to travel. Robert asked if I wanted to go to Patagonia, said that seemed to be more my style, a rugged terrain on the edge of the earth. Somehow it seemed a fitting place to reveal what we meant to each other, how far we would go for the other. On the shores of Last Hope Sound, in a hotel that resembled a hobbit house, I asked if Robert had thought any more about my proposal.

"This is not the place to talk about that." His words were embittered and costly. A warning to keep away from such a guarded place. I receded from him. It seemed we were the only people for miles.

We tramped around Chilean Patagonia, driving dirt roads across the border to Argentina. The border agent was not keen to let us in. It took many proddings from the young attendant for him to come to the front desk. When he finally arrived more than an hour later, hungover and red with fury, there was a palpable threat in his mannerisms.

In an austere landscape marked only by the occasional herd of sheep, Robert and I drove for hours. We were lost in the wilderness. When the brilliant emerald waters of Lago Argentino came into view, we felt the thrill once again of being found, and the color revived in our eyes, something deep therein rekindled.

A few days later we were back in Chile, under the cathedral mountains of the towers in Torres del Paine. I decided there that I would indeed live my dream to climb mountains. In that spiritual moment under those towering stones, I came to the understanding that I was finally ready to climb.

Back home in Seattle, as I began to research climbing schools, I mused whether it was better to walk away from my life with Robert.

Something kept me there. Perhaps it was my history of running away and my desire to move beyond my previous limitations; perhaps I was creating a new map for my life; perhaps true love stays. I told myself that even if Robert ultimately decided he didn't want a future with me, at least I could learn how to have a healthy relationship. No one knows the future, so I practiced patience and a deep gratefulness for the present moment. As I began my yearlong course with a local mountaineering organization, I told myself that my dreams were possible. I would climb toward them.

The training was challenging. People kept dropping out of the program. Months went by. My relationship with Robert went on autopilot. In my awareness of the present, I began to realize that I was becoming a fixture, something reliable in his life yet not fully seen. We were living the life of a long-married couple, but there was no commitment. In flagrant attempts to wake Robert up, I asked him to focus on us. There was always an excuse. Work was demanding. He would get around to it. But I began to see his excuses as aversions. Were these aversions also my own? I fell back to the Portugal dilemma: Was I thankful, or had I started pretending?

I've always disdained being forced to do anything, and I spurn ultimatums, but I needed an answer. A major character flaw of mine, this disdain for ultimatums that I end up giving. I asked Robert to describe what I was to him, what future he saw with me in his life.

Days before my Rainier climb, Robert truncated our relationship. He was finally able to say he did not see a future with me in it. With such perfect, ill timing, I moved two hours away from the home Robert had bought in Seattle and into a cottage I purchased on an island that was supposed to be our retreat from the city, a house whose previous owner had recently killed himself because he had lost his lifelong love. He was only sixty. "They didn't tell you?" my new neighbor said, with a grief-stricken face.

The scars of that love were incised in the remains of my new home. The whole house reeked of nicotine, door frames were cracked and scraped from the wife's walker on her long road out of this life, and there was a brand-new bathroom floor among faucets with fixtures falling apart.

The other neighbor was still scarred by the actions of the previous owner. "He shot himself," practically whispered out of the mouth of a recent widower, who wondered aloud if we are all destined for such a fate. And here I was, a first-time homebuyer, heartbroken myself, in a home with a history as recent and raw as my breakup. In those first nights, clutching my dog on a lone mattress in an empty room, I begged the resident ghosts to have mercy on me, because I too was grief-stricken. For better or for worse, I was staying in the campsite they had abandoned.

To cope, I joked with myself that I had moved into Hemingway's final home, and as a writer it was my job to turn this box of bullshit into something beautiful, for me, for my ex, and for the previous tenant and his wife.

Only a few months before, Robert and I had been in New Zealand, in Christchurch, the devastation from a past earthquake still visible six years later. It is strange that a different quake from 2011 is still felt in our lives. Like the Christchurch quake on a minor scale, there was a lost love, a great devastation that had created the conditions in which Robert and I existed today.

Before I knew how to love myself, I had fallen in love with a gregarious man who garnered the affection of those he encountered. But Orion, my boyfriend at the time, didn't love himself either. From the start, we were a spiraling dance of comets, careening through the night, coming closer together, pushing each other apart. He was my first true love. "You and me versus the world," he promised. I relinquished control. Our passion burned brightly, and there was much risk. After a year and a half together, and having just moved into a new apartment together, he left me at the start of a snowstorm. I listened to Bon Iver's album *For Emma, Forever Ago* repeatedly, unable to see out the windows of my apartment or out of my hazy eyes. Months went by. Sporadically Orion would return, swearing that I was the only one, that we just couldn't live together right now. But the borrowed car wasn't his. I knew there was someone else.

They say we accept the love we think we deserve, so I finally said goodbye to Orion. Some years later he came to me, looking for a salve for his heartache. He told me all about Robert. As he told the story, I put all the missing puzzle pieces into their places. Unknowingly, he confessed that Robert was the one he had been seeing all those months while I lived alone in the apartment we had moved into together. Robert was the one Orion left me for.

The last stop in New Zealand was Kaikōura, a place of catastrophe from an earthquake just weeks before. We were barely able to get there, driving roads that crumbled to dust below us and nearly broke our rental car. There in the destruction, in a vacant tourist town, we spent our last night overseas. New Zealand was our last international trip together. The roads washed into the sea.

On our final night together, sitting in the house I had helped refashion, I asked Robert, "Why did you pursue me so fervidly if you weren't sure? You knew I wasn't open to you after Orion." The emotional frustration muddled my thoughts and words. "I wasn't in that place. You have no idea how hard it was for me to find the forgiveness in my heart to open myself up to loving you. And now, you break up with me."

My words were barely audible between the tumult. The sifting of two storylines into one. You only ever see the true story from the end. If great love does indeed grow from deep sorrow, my soul is fertile for its roots.

"I'm so sorry," was all he could say. With little ceremony, he abdicated my love, our life together.

The next day the great birch tree in his backyard fell. He said to write that down, a poetic finish. It said all that we could not.

The night before the climb up the volcano, I read Thich Nhat Hanh's *How to Love*, a gift given by his concerned friend, Amy, after we returned from Paris, and the aftermath of an unrequited proposal. Like me, she was a remnant of Orion's life, now made Robert's. I am now a remnant of both.

The book spoke of loving lightly and letting go of those not meant for you, of leaving no impact, and of other noble pursuits in life. This was the second time I had read the book, and I returned to it hoping to find some wisdom in the uncertainty.

Although I respect its edicts of letting go, I find an all-too-similar point of connection in its philosophy and my ex-lovers. The book says to let go if it doesn't work perfectly. My lovers let go because it didn't feel right.

As I slowly put this broken house on the island together, alone, nothing feels right. I wonder how many times I'll put someone else's house back together again, only to have to leave. The last time I was alone on a mattress on the floor was when Orion left me for Robert. Hemingway and the last tenant come to mind. Heartbreak multiplied. Heartbroken, heartsick, a single man living in a two-bedroom apartment. This has happened before.

As I stand on the edge of this volcano, nothing feels right, and yet I still climb.

Orion had said he couldn't be with me because I wanted to get married, that I lived in a fantasy world. It's true, for years I wanted to get married while it wasn't legal. I fought for our right to get married. Not one moment of that felt right. Robert said he couldn't see a future with me because I wanted children, and he wasn't sure this was a world that supports two dads raising kids.

But few parts of my experience as a gay man in this world have felt supportive. And yet I persist.

This climb doesn't feel comfortable. Just because I can't see the summit doesn't mean it's not there. I bristle at the idea that things come naturally to everyone. My life has been a struggle and upward battle against forces greater than me. The idea that things will simply fall into place and feel right, to me, is an idea riddled with privilege. Things don't just happen. We must act. We must try. And we can't do it alone. The cleanup doesn't come easy. It doesn't feel nice. I would never have loved Robert were it not for the hard cleanup I did in the aftermath of Orion. In the alpine landscapes of my heart, I have much stewardship to do if I am to attempt a summit with another.

At base camp, by the ranger station at Camp Schurman last night, I imagined a man who will reach the summit with me. As prayer flags rippled with the wind and a trio of hummingbirds flitted about in the alpine air, the idea struck a chord within me. Maybe it's not just about one peak but the ability to keep climbing, because there are many peaks.

On the summit of Mount Rainier, the wind rages. The newborn sun blinds the eye. My imagination had me expecting grand vistas, epic sights, but from this height the most notable features are the other volcanoes sitting in their solitude, spread out in their towering loneliness. The view from up here is desolate, otherworldly. It seems a place of deep meditation, a plain between-space. What I thought would be a crowd of jubilant people is instead a mass of exhausted faces leaning downward, shoulders heavy. Instead of lingering at the top, most climbers hurriedly leave the summit, more than happy to begin the descent.

At the climax of my relationship with Robert, he whispered these words to me: "Until you, every breakup I've had was because of substance use or abuse. I didn't know people could break up from a healthy relationship."

I thought our breakup was respectable, and for the first time in my life I thought I could maintain a friendship after the break. But when I was ready to start dating again, Robert served me with a lawsuit, suing me for custody of my dog Buoy and monetary compensation for his role in caring for my dog. We turned into a kind of millennial melodrama. Even though I had written proof that Robert admitted Buoy was mine and mine alone, I still had to find a lawyer willing to take up a case that fell under animal rights law and not divorce law, though we were never married. Robert hired the only lawyer in the region who represented animal rights cases, and it took me months to research and find a lawyer who could counter Robert's outlandish claims. He would ultimately drop his lawsuit after my lawyer said we'd countersue for partial ownership of Robert's million-dollar house. Part of the final agreement was that he would drop his lawsuit if I didn't sue him, with the caveats that we could never talk to each other again or Robert would take Buoy from me legally, and that if I died he, not my current partner, would get custody of my dog. It felt like a violent end, an eruption.

As I climb into the future, I try to remember the biggest impact Robert had on me, in a moment with my mother. She had grown accustomed to telling people that "one of the worst days of my life was when Lance told me he's gay." She'd say it offhandedly, like it was something she'd gotten over. Every time she said it, it felt like a whip had lashed my heart. It hurt all the more because of everything that had happened with my father and baby brother, and how she put my identity on the same level as that horror and loss. But I stayed silent. The first time Robert heard her say it, his jaw fell loose, and he looked at me with a pain that felt similar to what I carried but of which I never spoke. I looked away in shame. For weeks afterward, he couldn't stop talking about it. The next time we saw my mom, she said it again. "You know, one of the worst days of my life was the day Lance told me he's gay."

"How dare you say that?" Robert said, his voice full of fury. "Do you have any idea what your son has been through?"

She never said those words again.

Perhaps, instead of leaving no trace, we can try to leave the campground better than we found it. Leaving no trace simply isn't good enough for our generation, good enough for our relationships, or for the earth. So much damage has already been done, so much baggage and trash are already strewn about our lives.

It's not about the peak entirely; it's also about the exhausted moments where you stop to take a break, to see a view you might never see again: the first birth of light from sunrise, a stray comet that lights up the night which you alone notice, the morning star far behind, a white glacier burning pink at dawn. Those were more beautiful than the summit to me. It's about the waypoints at base camp, where you pick up other people's trash and strangers tie down your tent when the wind is raging and you're not there to do it yourself. It's about overcoming your own capabilities, pushing past the hardest moments of your life, and continuing, not just for yourself but for everyone else on your rope team.

And it's not just about the summit but also the long way down, the long way out. And it's not just about this climb.

Maybe loving is about being a good steward, one who doesn't own but rather cares as they are able to. Because it's not my mountain; it was their house before I moved in; and he was never my man, although I'll always be a part of their stories. In all this change, I'll try to leave my trace, a cleaner campsite, loving memories for those whose paths I cross, and words that may last longer than my footsteps. I can only hope to contribute in such a way—to love with gratitude, not to pretend, and to honor the days. My first mountain taught me that.

There are always other mountains, and maybe, just beyond this vantage point, someone who wants to climb them.

Our Nature

Less than half a mile into my hike, I confront a broken bridge over the surging Canyon Creek, which today looks more like a raging river. After removing my shoes and tying them to my pack, I wade barefoot into the heavy flow of frigid water. The unexpected heat wave has melted the snowfields and glaciers of these North Cascades peaks and has made fording this waterway a near impossibility. For more than an hour, I attempt to route-find my way through the heavy folds of water that nearly push my feet from under me. If I lose my balance, this fifty-pound pack will make it difficult to keep myself from drowning. I walk back to my car, defeated. My goal today is to visit the site of Gary Snyder's first fire lookout on Crater Mountain, a trip I've planned for years, but every time I attempt it something happens to keep me from visiting this mythic site. At the trunk of my dusty car, I take off my pack and contemplate Snyder's words: "Some of us have learned much from traveling day after day on foot over snowfields, rockslides, passes, torrents, and valley floor forests, by 'putting ourselves out there.'... For those who would seek directly, by entering the primary temple, the wilderness can be a ferocious teacher." His words ring true in this moment.

I open the trunk and see a second pair of old shoes that have been sitting there, forgotten, from some unknown time frame.

They become an answer. With a newfound determination, I put my pack back on and for the second time hike to the creek.

The shoes on my feet allow me to counter the weight of the water. It climbs past my waist as I use every bit of strength to lean into the river, using both walking poles to keep me from falling forward. It's over in a matter of minutes, and I find myself soaked and covered in forest humus. After rinsing the soil off my clothes and changing to my dry hiking boots, I stow the wet shoes in a hollow stump and hike up to the intersection of the much longer trail.

An hour or so into the main trail, I come across a group of young folks practically running down the path. They are shocked to see that I am alone. I ask them if they came over the pass, and they say they intended to hike up and over it, but the mosquitoes were so bad that they are giving up.

"Where are you going?" a young girl asks me.

"To camp on Crater Mountain."

Her face conveys shock. "Alone?" she says. "It's not safe. And you'll be eaten alive!"

I assure her I'll be fine and that I do this sort of thing on a regular basis, but her expression is incredulous, even worried.

A few miles uphill I come across trails of trash on the dirt path. I start picking it up, first foil wrappers and plastic baggies, but soon the detritus gets larger and heavier. There are dirty socks and large packages with freeze-dried meals inside. It's likely that this trash came from the group I just passed, and the thought angers me. Why would anyone come to this wild place and leave their trash to mar it? Because there is so much trash, I tell myself I'll pick up the larger items on my return, so I don't have to carry other people's trash up the mountain and back down again.

Swarms of mosquitoes bite my skin, the ninety-degree heat is oppressive, and this steep climb has turned into a muggy bushwhack. I push through overgrown brush and bramble, my skin scratched and torn. Why do I do this to myself? I used to think it was about the summit, about standing on a distant peak as I overlooked ranges of mountains on all sides. Those moments are glorious, but there's more to my determination to push through this discomfort. To me, these climbs are reminiscent of my life story. So many obstacles have been in my path as I've searched for a place to call my own, on my way to an authentic life of self-acceptance and openness.

I've written before about how I found myself in this wild place. The books *The Dharma Bums* and *Desolation Angels* filled me with daydreams of mountaintops and enlightenment. Kerouac's words brought this land to life for me and inspired me to see it for myself. But what I didn't acknowledge at the time was that Kerouac was inspired by his character Japhy Ryder, based on his friend and outdoor mentor Gary Snyder. It was only through my close reading and research of Kerouac's process that I came to discover that Kerouac wasn't the dedicated environmentalist and outdoorsman he presented in his books; these passions were instead the ripples spread out from Snyder's influence on his life. While Kerouac's time in wild places eventually dwindled and he did not maintain a connection to it, Snyder spent the days of his life heralding the spiritual importance of a deep connection to wildness. At the moment of this writing, Snyder breathes this message still, and at the glorious age of ninety-five he is a steadfast embodiment, for all of us, of a life lived in equilibrium with the land that births us. A decade ago Kerouac brought me into this wilderness. But Gary Snyder taught me how to have a relationship with it. In *The Practice of the Wild*, he states that "self-realization, even enlightenment, is another aspect of our wildness—a bonding of the wild in ourselves to the (wild) process of the universe."

I make it to the glacial cirque and pristine Crater Lake to set up camp amid newly surging waterfalls. While the creek I had to cross at the start of this hike presented a difficult obstacle, the heat melting these glaciers has presented me with a magical surge of freshwater that falls on three sides of the cirque. The sound is ethereal, reverberating across the expanse. There isn't another human soul in this region right now. No tents or human sounds of any kind.

Here I am, among many facets, a gay man doing it all on his own. To me, this climb is a metaphor for queer existence in our time. Not only must we discover our identities and find self-reliance, but we must also do so in context with our time and place. We are out route-finding new trails, new ways of being. Often, we are the first ones to embark on a new path. My own path has so often felt isolated. The solitude in this cirque feels oddly comfortable, a home of my own.

A ridge a few hundred feet above the lake is the perfect spot to set up camp. I drop my pack, and the mosquitoes begin biting. In record time I set up my tent and climb inside to find refuge from the hungry teeth of these insects. The sun began its descent hours ago, and here I sit, accosted by swarms of relentless bloodsuckers. I watch as they strive to get through the mesh fabric under my rainfly. It doesn't look like I will make it to the summit, but I tell myself that it's okay—a successful excursion into nature doesn't require standing on top of a peak. With that surrender, I decide to continue walking in hopes of finding a nice ledge a thousand feet higher on the south ridge of Crater Mountain, halfway from this camp to my original destination. My new goal is to find a ledge where I can eat my dinner and watch the sun set behind the North Cascades ranges. From the moment I exit the tent, the mosquitoes land on me five times faster than I can squash them into bloody marks with my palm.

I've searched high and low for like-minded people in society. That search has often yielded scanty results, with few easily identifiable standard-bearers of the openly gay type. Recently in my journeys I found a self-identifying queer environmentalist, Robert Moor, and his work struck a chord in me. In Moor's wandering opus, *On Trails*—a meditation on what trails mean for humanity—he asks the question, Why do we hike? His proposed answer: "I believe what we hikers are seeking is simplicity—an escape from civilization's garden of forking paths." His offering seems legitimate to me. In my years of walking through wilderness, I've returned time and time again for the separation it grants from the frenetic obligations of my life. There is so much noise in my daily life, so many options, so many choices with unknown outcomes. It becomes difficult to make decisions. Out here in the wild the noise softens, and I can see through it, down to a more simplified version of the task at hand. Whether that task is the question of how to exist as a gay man, how open to be in my life and career, and how to accept the world as it is at this moment, all the while reaching for and working toward a better world for tomorrow, these topics are not easy to confront. The hard but rewarding hours on trails give me a moment to catch my breath, center myself, and make decisions about my life.

As I reach the west-facing ridgeline I had planned to eat my dinner on, I realize that I might have enough time to scramble to the summit, which is only eight hundred feet higher. I stop to catch my breath and wipe sweat from my brow. The mosquitoes start biting again. So much for stopping for dinner. I'd be the one eaten. I continue upward and make it to a strange maze of boulders that I climb up using my hands and feet. There are painted yellow X's to guide the scrambling route; a variety of yellow and orange fungus grows on the rock and is brighter than the faded paint. I climb up the wrong route, realize I'm in a precarious position, climb back down to a yellow X, multiple times without success. Daylight drains from the sky. The sun seems to be inches from the horizon. If I don't find the route soon, I'll have to turn back.

I've been pushing against this climb all day. The hike started with a difficult river crossing. It's been oppressively hot, the bugs have been murderous, and here I hang from the side of this peak, alone and incapable of summiting. It all feels so pointless. What am I doing here? A faint but cooling alpine wind passes over my skin, and I realize no mosquitoes are biting me at this elevation. I look up, see the next X, and climb toward it. After that one I see the next, and all the remaining X's until I climb out of the steep cliffs and onto a magnificent meadow that ambles easily toward the summit. I walk the welcoming ridgeline, held aloft in a supreme state of softness. The fading sunlight changes the world's color to a brilliant amber.

At the highest point I find a steel post that once held the legendary fire lookout. A glint catches my eye. I am standing on shattered and melted fragments of glass. I squat down and pick one up. Its smooth and sharp contours sit lightly in my hand. It must be the glass from the lookout, melted time and time again by lightning strikes from the winter storms that rage against these peaks. I look out to the many-layered mountains that encompass this place and feel at once timeless and firmly grounded to this mortal moment. I can hardly believe I made it to the top. The reward of standing silently in these primordial mountains as the sun sets is nearly unfathomable.

In this deep mountaintop meditation, I ponder Gary Snyder's words: "The wilderness pilgrim's step-by-step breath-by-breath walk up a trail, into those snowfields, carrying all on the back, is so ancient a set of gestures as to bring a profound sense of body-mind joy. . . . The point is to make intimate contact with the real world, real self. . . . The wilderness as a temple is only a beginning. . . . The best purpose of such studies and hikes is to be able to come back to the lowlands and see all the land about us, agricultural, suburban, urban, as part of the same territory—never totally ruined, never completely unnatural. It can be restored."

Robert Moor said, "It may sound strange (even sacrilegious) to some, but in a very real way, wilderness is a human creation." In *On Trails*, he tells a story of when he went on an urban hike along a highway with the perpetual hiker Nimblewill Nomad. Nimblewill's given name is Meredith J. Eberhart. Now in his mid-eighties, he's been walking nonstop for decades and has written books about it. Moor recounts that during his hike with Nimblewill, the fabled walker said the problem "was that hikers tended to divide their lives into compartments: wilderness over here, civilization over there. 'The walls that exist between each of these compartments are not there naturally,' he said. 'We create them. The guy that has to stand there and look at Mount Olympus to find peace and quiet and solitude and meaning—life has escaped him totally! Because it's down there in Seattle, too, on a damn downtown street. I've tried to break those walls down and decompartmentalize my life so that I can find just as much peace and joy in that damned homebound rush-hour traffic that we were walking through yesterday.'"

This idea that I can find the same feeling I have standing atop this mythical mountaintop as I have at home is something I only am recently beginning to understand. I live in a dense wood that blocks out the sun for most of the daylight hours. Yet in that shaded forest I've found a wilderness teeming with life: the patterns and habits of our local coyote family; the aviary bustle of barred owls, bald eagles, robins, and osprey; the patterns of the subterranean moles across the field; and the rabbits and squirrels that scavenge for food. In quiet moments, slowly walking or standing among the trees, I've found feelings that are in line with what Snyder calls "intimate contact with the real world." I've had those same touches of clarity, though far rarer, on the street corners of downtown Seattle while I work as an EMT administering care to unhoused citizens who find shelter in tents. The kindness of a toothless smile, and all that an individual had to overcome in order to share that kindness, is a marvel I don't quite know how to decipher. Could this practice of the wild that I partake of, out here in this rough and enlightening wilderness, be taken home to a way of life that can be practiced on the daily commutes and obligations of my habitual existence?

As the sun sets, I climb down toward my camp and rehydrate my freeze-dried dinner with cold water on the move, because the mosquitoes have not gone to sleep yet. I pull out my headlamp and place it on my sweaty forehead as the darkness makes following the path to camp that much harder. When I finally reach my tent, the night is black and smeared with the brilliant stars of the Milky Way.

In the morning I wake up to swarms of mosquitoes that assault the netting of my tent, waiting for me to exit and give them breakfast. As I watch the feral behavior of those insects, I eat an oatmeal bar and make a cold instant coffee. This is my moment of peace today, so I listen to the sound of water falling from the cliffs outside. I know that the moment I exit the tent it will be a mad dash to gather all my gear and crash down the mountain. In comedic fashion, I stumble through the act of packing up my camp and stuffing it in my backpack, as my skin gets bitten by hordes of insect mouths.

On my descent I realize that though I often come here for peace, I don't always find it. Instead I find challenge, awareness of this often uncomfortable present moment, the feeling of being dangerously and vibrantly alive, even on the edge of mortality. I find callouses and blisters, rashes of bug bites, and bodily exhaustion. And in that catharsis I find release, acceptance, and gratefulness to be alive. I also find my limits, my faults, and more questions. On my way down, I don't take the trash I pass for the second time. Exhausted, skin-flushed, drenched with two days of sweat, and covered in bite marks, I can't gather the strength to pick up the damage others have left. It weighs on me as a moral failing, and I feel immense guilt because I had been so pompous in my thinking yesterday. As I rush down the mountain toward the raging creek, I think of all the trash I've walked past in my life, trash I just left there. When I get back to my car, I realize I had the strength and the time to take it with me. Next time, I reinforce within myself, I will be better. I will care more for things other than myself. For me, that's the challenge of bigger issues like climate change; I need to care enough to make a change, to fix a problem that I might not have created but have been bequeathed because of the time and place I live in. This problem I've contributed to on a regular basis.

There's so much that my time in the wilderness has taught and continues to teach me. It's been an integral part of me finding a way through life as an openly gay man and has helped me overcome so many challenges. I want to share that with other queer people in hopes of showing them a way of life that's given so many people throughout history a sense of meaning and connection.

Back home, I reach out to Moor and ask him for his thoughts on queer people's relationship to nature. He writes back, "Queer people have a more difficult but potentially a more rewarding relationship with nature precisely because we are told from a young age that we are not natural. 'Nature' and the 'natural' are human concepts which are continually being redefined; we know this in our bones. This makes it easier for us to see how nature, too, is not as natural as it seems. Rather, it is deeply entangled with us. It creates us and we create it; it can heal us and we can heal it. And we have a lot of healing to do!"

A deep relationship to place can be a way out of our current climate crisis. For queer people, this relationship can offer a healing salve for the historical abuses inflicted upon us by societal structures and can promote a sense of purpose and connection in our existence here as a part of this environment. Snyder said that "self-realization, even enlightenment, is another aspect of our wildness," and he conveyed the accessibility of this self-realization for all people when he said, "A person with a clear heart and open mind can experience the wilderness anywhere on earth." We don't have to trek to remote mountaintops to experience this; we can simply walk out our front door and into this wild world.

To share this concept of wilderness with those who have little or no access to it, to help them care deeply for and connect with the environment, is a tool that can be used to heal the earth and ourselves. For queer people who have historically been excluded or erased from the "natural" world, a reclamation of our inherent nature and place in the cycles of the earth can be entwined with the return to a balanced environment. We can replace centuries of abuse and extraction with stewardship, sustainability, and community for all living beings. The answers to our greatest challenges are in our nature. I hope you go out there and find them.

Out in the Open

I've never seen a wall of fire like the one on the ridge in front of me, and our strike team of five brush trucks is driving right toward it. I'm in the truck at the front of the line, and my lieutenant tells me to grab the nozzle from the hose reel and climb on top of our vehicle. I put water on the fire as we slowly drive forward, with a wet bandana wrapped around my mouth to protect my lungs from the thick smoke.

Just over the fire line I see another wall of fire barreling toward us. There isn't much time to react, so I climb down and rush to the roadside as the two fronts merge into one. A wave of fire crests over my head and around me on all sides. The wind howls and pushes the water back at me. I choke on the thick smoke and heat, my eyes burning with black tears. My hose stream can't compete; I'm nearly engulfed by fire. Just as I feel it overcoming me, it burns its fuel of sagebrush and grass and dampens just enough for me to beat it into submission. We fight all night.

The next day we gather at a viewpoint above the Grand Coulee Dam, in central Washington on the Columbia River, just below the plateau where the fire had been the night before. The two other Seattle-based firefighters and I wait for the rest of our strike team, comprising firefighters from across Washington state. We laugh about how close to death we were last night, trying to shake off the stress. "You've got real grit," my officer says warmly, a stark change from his usual gruff demeanor. "I want you to know that if anything comes up while we're out here, we've got your back."

He's referring to the fact that I'm openly gay. By now, my whole department knows back home, and I've been wondering how this would come up while we're out here. "Yeah, we have your back," the other firefighter says. I assume he's referring to the possibility of a fight. When I was in the Navy in the late 2000s, this would happen occasionally—some random guy would take offense to my sexuality and threaten violence. Their spoken support is profound to me and makes me feel like I'm part of a team out here. In places like this, you can't afford to be on your own.

The rest of the strike team makes it to the overlook. A brash young firefighter takes a serious turn to tell a story about how some locals near Colville, Washington, pulled automatic rifles on a group of firefighters and forced them off their land. The story reminds me of my own time near Colville.

Deep in the Colville National Forest, not too far from the Canadian border, my team and I fought the Bodie Mountain Fire in August 2016. We'd been covered in soot and dirt for days. I'd been put in charge of the pump at the local creek, to fill the water tenders as needed. As I sat by the creek and scribbled some poetry into my notebook, two local men stopped by to chat. They asked me where I was from, and when I told them Seattle, their tone became oppositional. "Those damn liberals and their big government."

It was clear: I had to tread carefully. I was alone, my crew miles away, and even though I had a radio and could call for help, it wouldn't have come for a long while. It felt like I was across enemy lines, by myself. I looked for a point of connection, and when they brought up the topic of guns I told them I had been a gunner in the Navy. This appeased them; they shared their respect for our armed forces.

Back at the dam, the brash young guy says the men who pulled rifles on the firefighters are now in prison. I wonder, if I had been honest about who I was to those two guys in Colville, would they have run me off with rifles? For some of us, a potential danger is simply being open about who we are.

Since I was a kid, I've wanted to go off into the unknown and explore. And I wanted to find people to model myself after. But I couldn't find any openly gay guys that fit my vision. Without someone charting the way, I began to wonder: Was the great outdoors a place for me? Would I be safe being a visibly out adventurer?

When I was in the Navy during Don't Ask, Don't Tell, the only stories I heard about other openly gay people were cautionary tales about the dangers of being open, the cost of being truthful. When I began my firefighting career, the only stories I could find about openly gay people in this field were stories to beware of, how being open could cost you your career. When I started backpacking and climbing, I was happy not to hear so much about the dangers of being gay, but I still couldn't find any openly gay climbers to learn from.

While I've wanted mentors and role models, I've had to do without them. I've had to be creative and hopeful in my adventuring, always on the lookout for others like me, always eager to share what I've learned. Together we're mapping out what adventurous lives like ours can look like.

Alone in my Coupeville cottage on Whidbey Island, Buoy and I spend our days running the madrone-lined trails of Ebey's Landing National Historic Reserve. The sand and stone coastline along the Salish Sea and the Straits of Juan de Fuca are our playground. Most nights we watch the sunset together as it sets beyond the sight of land, in a narrow corridor that spans out to open ocean.

The population of Coupeville is under two thousand people, mostly retired or families. Deer graze in my yard and stop traffic in the quiet streets. I spend a lot of time at my kitchen table looking outside, watching the clouds pass over the face of Mount Baker and the sparse ships that make passage through Penn Cove. I've never had a view before, and I sit transfixed by it.

Few single people choose to move to small towns, yet here I am, a single, gay man in a small island town. Because of this reality, I've downloaded all the dating apps and spend too much time in conversation with people more than a hundred miles away. Most of my connections come from the north. The closest city is Vancouver, British Columbia, followed by Victoria. For months I chat with Canadian bachelors and make a few short trips in hopes for a future, but as with most online connections they all fall short.

Then, on the day before Thanksgiving, a handsome man named Oliver pops up in a nearby town. Incredulous, I assume he must be a tourist, but our conversation strides with ease, and soon he tells me he's visiting his mom in neighboring Port Townsend, a short ferry ride from me to the Olympic Peninsula. We attempt to meet up, but we both have family obligations for the holiday and can't seem to find the time. We keep talking, though; the rarity of our similarities ties us together immediately, even if we can't find a way to meet.

The next day is Thanksgiving, and after dinner my grandmother asks us all to gather around her in the living room. She has something to share with us. Tonight is the night. She will take the pill. This is goodbye.

I make it to the bathroom and stand at the vanity I have known my whole life, head down, my body a tripod supporting this ill attempt to center myself, to put on a good show. Behind me is a picture that has been there for years, yet one I've never fully noticed. On it, a lighthouse surrounded by rough seas bears the inscription "A friendly beacon on the shore reassures the soul." It somehow describes my forthcoming loss. I will no longer have my lighthouse. This sends a thrush of grief through my body. Sweat and tears form, but I cannot allow myself to release. As a first responder who has been with people on their deathbed, I know how vital these last moments are. There is a somber responsibility to be strong, to nurture a calm and peaceful atmosphere, not to instill fear or anxiety. These moments are all we have left, and we must make them count. Even in my swelling grief, I recognize the gift of having a goodbye.

I enter the living room of this modest three-bedroom rambler. It has been the headquarters of our family since I was a toddler. So many pictures of my siblings and cousins and me growing up here, eating cheese puffs on my grandfather's lap. He has long since passed but still holds a palpable space within these walls. In the living room, my family sits in a circle around our matriarch, Jacqueline, who goes by Jackie. To our surprise, a few months ago she was diagnosed with stage-four cancer in her breasts and uterus. Up to this point, she had been a healthy woman with all her faculties, and at eighty-five she has little interest in changing her quality of life just to labor through the next few months to a year in a hospital bed. She tells us she will take the pill tonight, so that she can end life on her terms. This sends reverberations through my family, shock and awe, and some disapproval. But it is her choice. There is so much grace in her decision, even in this emotional moment, so much poise in her ability to choose her path. As she sits on the couch in front of a wall of gold-spackled mirrors, she makes sure to look in everyone's eyes, hold their hands, tell them the best things about them, wish them specific successes unique to each person's needs and desires.

Whether purposefully emulated or just an inclination I picked up somewhere along the way, to me she resonates as a Jackie Kennedy type. With a short, silver bob of a haircut that is her trademark, naturally rosy cheeks, and a manner of movement that resembles royalty, she is the most dignified member of our family. Though I never said it aloud, I always thought of her as a queen—quick to correct a familial discrepancy, lavish in her application of approval when appropriately earned, prim and orderly and content to abide her time in her castle, never venturing too far away, always with an open door for an unexpected visit. But what is most noticeable about my grandmother is the enduring love she has for my grandfather, Jack, who died some twenty-eight years ago, when I was six.

She would tell us vivid stories about him at every holiday. Their love turned more into legend than memory for us grandkids. He had enlisted in the army during the Korean War and was stationed at an airbase in Germany. Although he didn't see combat and came home after his initial four years, it was in Europe where his love affair with airplanes began. My few memories of him were with airplanes, at the museum of flight and at the airport where we would go to watch the planes land and take off. While my grandfather was serving out his enlistment, Jackie was home working in downtown Seattle at the Olympic Hotel. The manager had given her a job as an accountant, a job she was woefully unskilled for. "I bet the next accountant had a time trying to balance those books," she said, her mischievous laugh stunning us grandkids. "Luckily, he thought I was pretty, so I got away with making up the numbers."

She told us stories about how different Seattle was back then. One could walk the empty streets in the evening, not a car in sight. On one fortuitous evening, the man she was seeing asked her to go on a double date with his Army buddy. It was at that dinner that Jackie met Jack, to the dismay of both their respective dates. After a brief courtship, they married and embarked on the idyllic American dream, had three girls and one boy, bought a house by a lake while my grandfather managed the supply at a grocery store and eventually started his own supply company, coaching my father's baseball team and hosting parties at the family home.

My grandmother was a stay-at-home mom, working hard to do her part and maintain their chosen lifestyle. When my grandfather died in his sixties from prostate cancer, my grandmother never let him go. It was like he was there next to her, always a part of the conversation, through the tears and the laughter of her recollection, the handsome pictures of his tan skin contrasting with the white of his teeth and hair. She was as much in love with him now, perhaps even more, than she was when he was alive.

Jackie's enduring love for my grandfather and for her family was perhaps her most beautiful trait, but in order to know how much she meant to me, you'd have to know a bit more about my immediate family, her son and my mother. They too married young and started their version of the idyllic American life. In contrast to the scarce involvement with the Catholic church that my grandparents had, my parents found their salvation in being born again and raised our family in an Independent Fundamental Baptist church. It was a simple life, a regimented mix of school and church with strict rules about clothing and influence. We were sheltered from the world outside our bubble of religion. All could have been well had it not been for my forbidden secret. I was a gay kid, and I knew it from an early age. The church spoke regularly about the evils of being a homosexual, and there was a very real threat of being sent away to a conversion camp if I were to ever say anything or be found out, so I lived in the shadows of my shame from a very young age. That was all I knew and all I ever expected to know.

But there was one sliver of light in that darkness which never left me. My grandmother pulled me aside one day. I must have been eight or nine, and she squatted down to my level. She looked me deep in the eye, which was something she had never done before.

"Lance, I want you to remember something," she said, as she put her hands on my small shoulders. "There is nothing wrong with being gay."

Those words. I wasn't quite sure what they meant, but they meant everything. I carried those words like a lifeline, a buoy that I clung desperately to in the wild waves of my youth and lack of culture. I carried them all the way until the day I actually believed them, so very far in the future that would be.

There is nothing wrong with being gay.

It's impossible for me to convey how important my grandmother's words were to me, and how they continued to show me love through the many following years, as I had to learn how to love myself. Those words meant everything. They still do, more than ever.

I eventually came out to my family, when I was twenty, after I left home and joined the Navy. My grandmother, my greatest ally, wasn't surprised in the least. She helped me navigate the reactions of family members who had major issues with my revelation. It took years to work through the vast differences between opposing views, but she was there the whole time, quietly encouraging me to rise above the noise and to remember that we are all family, that love is what matters most.

As I sit next to her on this final evening, she looks at me with an expression of awe and radiant affection. "You've gotten so much further in life than I ever imagined for you. I am so proud of what you have become," she says. In that moment I study her eyes, the blue depth of a northern ocean, as they well up with something so much more powerful than tears. When she speaks again with all the tenderness of unconditional love, she doesn't say my sailor, or my firefighter, or my grandson; she looks at me as if she knows exactly who I am deep down inside, and she states, "My author." Completely vulnerable and open, we look at each other for the last time, saying far more than words could ever attempt to in those fleeting moments that seem to last even now.

Life, like the sea, is full of storms. There are some people so full of light that they act as lighthouses for us, reminding us there is safe harbor if we continue through the storm, that someone is waiting for us to return. I've lost my grandmother, one of those lighthouses. The shore, the sea, is darker without her presence.

I'll try to emulate her, to become a light for others to be reassured by, because the light of her unconditional love still burns within me. What I've learned from her is that the light that you tend and share with the world can continue on even after you're gone. I love you, my darling Jackie. Thank you for lighting the way.

Back in Coupeville that night, I have dreams of my grandmother dying, of her reaching out for me because she can't breathe. Her grasping my arms for support. In the morning I get the official notice from my mother. She has passed.

This is the closest person to me who has died, and I feel the great chasm inside me that has opened and has no end. I feel like I need to go somewhere; I turn this way and that, go into this room and forget why, go into the living room and stand there for a time. I must go somewhere, but there is nowhere to go.

The man in Port Townsend, Oliver, texts me, and he gives me an anchor. I have work tomorrow, and he flies out in the morning, but we will both be in Seattle tonight and decide to grab a beer.

At the Thompson Hotel near Pike Place Market, in their rooftop bar the Nest, I walk in to see a tall man sitting on a stool near the floor-to-ceiling windows over Elliott Bay. When I sit down on the stool beside him, there's a relief that comes with a smile on both our faces. Our knees sit intertwined and occasionally touching. There's a magnetism and a familiarity that sets our conversation at ease.

And then his sister crashes the date.

She's hilarious and a jolt of energy, but I take it as a sign that the date isn't going well. It's getting late anyway, so I tell them I'll head back to my sailboat since I have work tomorrow. They both object and say we should order room service and have a sleepover, as they have a double hotel room for the night. How unconventional, a date that turns into a sleepover with his sister. If it were any other day, I would definitely say no thanks, but I don't want to be alone tonight, so I join them for a movie and late-night snacks in their room. We fall asleep, his sister on one bed, and two fully clothed men on the other. They're asleep before the movie ends, and I turn down the volume, roll over, and hold Oliver for the first time. It's a sweaty night. We sleep fully clothed, without much sleep, but here is the comfort I sorely needed. There's something deeper about this meeting, and it feels like family. How uncanny, to have lost someone so close to me earlier in the day and to feel like I gained someone so close later that night.

In the early morning I say goodbye to Oliver's sister, who is still in bed, and Oliver walks me down the hall. He invites me to come visit him in Manhattan Beach, California, and I say that I will. We kiss at the elevator, and I thank him for a night I needed. Work that day feels a bit more optimistic.

I buy a plane ticket to Los Angeles to visit him on my birthday in mid-December, but before I leave, I start to have second thoughts. My sister asks me what I'm so afraid of, and I say that I'm sick of putting time into relationships that will go nowhere. How could a long-distance relationship work? My plan is to stay at Oliver's house while I'm there. Essentially, I'll be staying at a stranger's house in a place I don't even like. LA was never my idea of a place I'd want to be. My sister tells me to grow up. I can always get a hotel room if it gets weird, and I have nothing to lose. "It's your birthday," she says. "Treat yourself."

So I do. I fly to LA with no expectations and the hope that the whole thing isn't a big mistake.

Oliver picks me up at the airport with his huge Great Dane, a harlequin with the coloring of a Dalmatian. He takes me to Terra Naya Resort for lunch on cliffs over the Pacific Ocean. A straight couple tells us that they love our little family. We're already getting mistaken for a couple. We linger in the ease of salt air and each other's company.

At his bachelor pad in Manhattan Beach, there's a suit of armor to greet us at the door. For a man who's been called Lancelot his entire life, I find it a serendipitous sign. The tiled loft of his living space feels like something I would design myself. The large fireplace with stacked firewood to the ceiling beside it, a large tree growing toward the loft ceiling, and the flotation ring with his last name on it all feel like a home I would create.

We walk six blocks to the beach, then walk the strand for a while before we get to town. At a restaurant with a view of the pier, we dine and talk of possibilities as the sun sets over the Pacific Ocean.

We start building a long-distance relationship. Since we live a thousand miles away from each other, we must travel whenever we want to spend time together. It takes a lot of effort, proving how invested we are in each other. We start meeting in various places—Yellowstone, Lake Tahoe, Desolation Sound—and regularly visit his cabin in Big Bear Lake and my cottage in Coupeville. We sail my boat in and around the waterways near Seattle and meet with friends on ski slopes across the West. Our lives together are centered around our time outside and our shared love for adventure.

For openly gay people outside, there's always that unknown part of the equation. What happens when something rare is made visible? Being openly gay in the great outdoors has at times made me feel more like a foreign tourist in our American wilderness than a citizen. And a few times it's felt dangerous.

But it also makes me feel that spirit of adventure. I get the chance to do something that might not have been done before, or simply to become one visible representation of nature's vivid diversity. For so long I wanted to see an openly gay man who fights wildfires, stands on the top of mythic peaks, and treks through forests so that I'd believe I could do the same. Now I've seen that man—I've become him. And I've learned that when we see the wild ranges of our earth as our own, we care more about them and desire to protect them.

If I weren't comfortable being openly gay in the great outdoors, then some of the most beautiful days of my life would never have happened.

After a bluebird day snowboarding in the French Alps in December 2018, Oliver told me there was something he wanted to show me. He took me down a steep trail and over a bridge with views of Mont Blanc, into a grove of larches, where a scene of lanterns and lighted letters spelled out the name our favorite song, "This Is It" by Scotty McCreery. He dropped down to one knee and asked me, "Will you live a great story with me?"

I joined him on one knee as photographers and families with laughing children at a nearby playground looked on. There, under a French Alps sunset, my new fiancé and I kissed and shared one of the most incredible moments of our lives in the place we love the most, nature.

Two years later, we sail the Salish Sea north toward the San Juan Islands during a pandemic, with an uncertain future and a menacing bank of wildfire smoke trailing behind us. In this dark period, we voyage toward a hopeful future. Our wedding in Whistler, British Columbia, has been rescheduled because the U.S.–Canadian border has been closed indefinitely. In our last-minute plan to elope, we forgot to get a marriage license, so we feverishly call every city hall in the region. Most are closed or on modified schedules because of the lockdowns, but we find one in Island County on Whidbey Island. A strange coincidence—

after recently selling my house in Coupeville, we must sail back to city hall, blocks away from the house, to sign for our marriage license.

Oliver moved to Seattle a few years ago and commuted to LA for work one week a month. We planned our wedding in Whistler, invited all our family and friends, but the pandemic hit and changed our plans. After rescheduling our wedding twice, we choose to marry secretly but hoped that we could still have our Whistler wedding in the future. We won't know at the time, but our wedding in Whistler will never happen, and the pandemic will be protracted for years.

Through the past few years with Oliver, it's been amazing to witness the sea change in my mother, who openly tells him, "I love you, my son-in-love." It's as if her eyes have been opened to this long journey that I've been on, this tireless push toward love. After all this time, all this growth, it's bittersweet that she won't get to come to the wedding of a love that's taken her so long to accept. But the knowledge alone that she would attend the ceremony fills me with something I never knew I missed. We've come such a long distance together, overcome so many tragedies and heartbreaks. For me, she's become a symbol of enduring love, one that has overcome so many ideological boundaries centuries in the making. She is a symbol of what is possible, despite our differences, when we truly love one another.

The marina supervisors have saved the end slip of the guest pier, a courtesy they told me they could not promise and rarely grant, but today all things align in our favor and we moor our sailboat at the end of the long wooden pier. It gives us the perfect vantage point to see the whole marina and a great runway for us to walk down to start the ceremony.

After we string up lights with the halyards of the sails, twilight begins and the smoke from the wildfires changes colors and feels more like the comfortable fog we are accustomed to in this seafaring region.

"Greetings, everyone! Welcome, Lance and Oliver and Buoy and Tahoe. We are here to honor and legalize the commitment that Lance and Oliver make to marry."

Our officiant, Michelle, is a woman we've never met. I found her on the county's listing of certified officiants. It described her as a librarian, and that connection to words was enough for me. As our dogs, Tahoe and Buoy, walk freely around the pier, they gaze at the fish that surround the boat. A blue heron screeches and swoops near the bow. The great bird interrupts the ceremony, but Michelle assures us that the fish and the heron are blessings from Poseidon. I like her immensely.

She opens a worn copy of Walt Whitman and begins to read: "'We two boys together clinging, One the other never leaving, Up and down the roads going—North and South excursions making, Power enjoying—elbows stretching—fingers clutching, Arm'd and fearless—eating, drinking, sleeping, loving, No law less than ourselves owning—sailing, soldiering—air breathing, water drinking, on the turf or the sea-beach dancing, Fulfilling our foray.' Thank you, Walt Whitman, for those beautiful sentiments. Oliver, Lance, today you are not surrounded by your family, friends or colleagues. In this secret ceremony you are blessed to be together and looking forward in what is such a hard time. This terrible pandemic that has taken so many lives, has disrupted so many others. Your plans for a big ceremony had to be changed. Yet today you are joyous and grateful.

"In this private ceremony you are here beneath the wind and the weather, above the waves, standing aboard this secure vessel *All' Swell*. Marriage has been a sacrament of society for thousands of years. Only recently has this sacrament been made available to two men who love each other. Sacrament means a sacred blessing. We know that legal marriage confers rights and responsibilities.

You chose the responsibilities along with the rights. You want to raise children. Such a beautiful wish! To take the responsibility to raise a child with love and protection and encouragement, to vow to stay together to create a home for the next generation to grow. Oliver, please share your vows with Lance."

Oliver stands with his back to the pier facing the sea and says, "You are everything I have ever dreamed of in another human being. You are kind, honest, creative, driven, and compassionate. You are the most beautiful person I have ever known. I am forever changed because of who you are and what you mean to me. I'm elated that you've chosen me to be your husband, and I promise to make you smile and laugh for the rest of our lives. Also, I promise to hold off secretly watching our Netflix shows until we are together. I promise to cuddle you as much as I do Tahoe and Buoy and pick up treats for you whenever they get some too. I promise to learn and practice your near impossible recycling methods. If Covid evolves into a zombie situation and you turn into one, I promise to let you bite me, so I too can be one and, therefore, stay by your side forever. Most of all, Lance, I promise to love you and to care for you wholly and infinitely. Our commitment today to each other is authentic and extraordinary—and best of all, it's all ours! You and me, Lance! This is our time, now and for always. Babe, this is it!"

Michelle laughs and guides me. "Lance, please share your vows with Oliver."

I face Oliver and notice spectators gathering along the pier. "It might sound crazy to some," I say, "to get married in a pandemic, with wildfires burning our region and unrest sweeping the globe. But I view this moment as an act of faith, in each other and in existence, an act of hope despite all that stands in our way. So, in this moment of profound hope, I promise to love you until I leave this earth. I promise to nurture and grow my patience, so that I can be a better partner through the challenges of life, to hold onto my hope, to let it shine bright in the best of times, and to hold the flame steady in the darkest of hours. I promise that I will always take care of myself, so that I am better capable of helping you. But I promise to also let you take care of me when I am weak. As I will care for you when you are depleted. I promise to always work toward a healthy, balanced relationship, where we can follow our own pursuits and grow stronger in the passions that we share. I promise to always work on us. To never grow entitled and ungrateful for the miracle of our love. To never stop learning about you, to listen to your thoughts, to ask about your day and your work, and to always see you for who you are and not who anyone else wants you to be. And finally, I promise to change with you through the seasons of life. To hold your hand on this long walk, and to always be your anchor as we sail through these adventures. You are my only one. I love you, Oliver."

"To formalize your union, you make vows to each other. Under the heavens, these promises endure. May you keep your promises. Lance, do you choose to marry Oliver?"

"I do."

"Oliver, do you choose to marry Lance?"

"Yes!"

"I now pronounce you married. You may kiss!"

As we kiss, the crowd cheers. The docks are full of joyful strangers who come to the end of the pier to celebrate with us. They say how much they support our love, are grateful for it in this socially distant time. It's a remarkable thing, to have come all this way and have struggled for so long in the communities I've traveled in, to be here now, surrounded by the love and support of complete strangers, here in the embrace of my husband.

Epilogue
A River Freed

Big leaf maples blush with the first bloom of autumn on the Olympic Peninsula. Just beyond the parking lot, the Elwha River rushes north toward the Strait of Juan de Fuca. A gate closes off the road, which once led to a ranger station. Although I was expecting the first big storm of the season, the sky is now blue, so I stow my rain gear. Signs warn me about bears and a cougar that has been seen in the area. As a solo hiker, I'll need to make noise along the way.

Not far along the road I find the closed National Park Center, eerily quiet. Staffing issues here too. The mists of recent rains evaporate from the roofs like smoke from burning buildings. It feels as if the landscape is swallowing up all traces of a park. This pallor of decay adds to my general sense of unease.

Four miles beyond, I come to the site of a former dam. At the end of the walkway the concrete ends abruptly. Two hundred feet below, the river cuts between the broken walls of the dam, rampaging below the steep cliffs of Glines Canyon. I lean out over the railing and feel the exhilaration of the sheer drop and the roar of a river freed.

The dam destruction project began in September 2011—the biggest removal in U.S. history. That same month, I was preoccupied with another historic removal, the repeal of Don't Ask, Don't Tell.

In an interview, my favorite poet, Gary Snyder, recommended *The Account*, written by Álvar Núñez Cabeza de Vaca, published in 1542. He said it gave the clearest picture of what this continent looked like before the colonizers came.

It began a new journey for me.

As one of the first European explorers, Cabeza de Vaca came to North America from Spain to document a supposed New World. Starting on the shores of Florida, he ventured deep into the unknown, traveling through the lands of the Indigenous people. He was astonished by the different cultures and traditions he witnessed. As I read his account, I was thrilled to see a version of this land I'd never encountered. It was so strange and distant that I felt like an explorer myself. I was step for step with him in discovery until I read this line: "I saw one wicked thing, and that was a man married to another man."

This judgment—so commonplace, so arrogant—defined much of my life. Even in a distant time period, on the same continent where I've grown up nearly half a millennium later, there was this tension between one rigid ideology and another more accepting one.

I was immediately interested in these two men, this hidden history I had never encountered. As I researched more, I learned that the men were documented by other explorers. They would become known as two spirits—men who dressed outside of gender norms, carried heavy loads, participated in war parties, and were respected spiritual leaders, all while living with and marrying other men.

Western civilization has been documenting homosexuality for centuries, much of it weighed down with ideological judgment.

But these two men lived beyond its reach in a way that is hard to imagine now.

Half a millennium after their time, I'm trekking through the wilds of the Cascade Range, across Sulphide Glacier toward the peak of Mount Shuksan, on the ancestral lands of the Nooksack people. This is my first mountaineering expedition, and Shuksan will be my second ascent of the journey. My body is weary, blistered, and chafed from days of toil. But my mind is clear and free.

A brilliant full moon illuminates the snowy landscape, so I turn off my headlamp to soak in the celestial glow. I'm roped in with two other climbers, and two other teams are ahead of us. All of their headlamps point down. With my head up, I scan the expansive cirque that we move through and the dark stone pyramid before us. I'm overcome with a deep sense of spirituality. This place is sacred. It feels as if we have stepped outside of time itself. It brings tears of wonder to my eyes.

This moment on this glacier—the fullness of the moon, the deep intimacy with an intoxicating alpine landscape—assures me that I am where I need to be, that I am natural. I grew up along the shorelines of the Salish Sea, only eighty miles from this summit. This is my home.

I have not always known this feeling.

From early childhood, I was taught that people like me were an unnatural part of the landscape, alien and unwanted. Raised in a fundamentalist tradition, I was told there was no place for my kind. This realization would become ever more pressing as I forged my own path in the world, trying to move beyond the ideological limits of my youth.

On our ascent to the summit, Robin Wall Kimmerer's words from *Braiding Sweetgrass* come to me like a prayer: "To be native to a place we must learn to speak its language." I've been searching for that feeling, a deep knowing and connection to a place.

As a gay man in a straight world, as a white man descended from immigrant people on a continent that was not our own, as a sailor traveling restlessly across the globe ever in search of home, I know little of what a deep connection to place can feel like.

But in this cirque, I am beginning to.

On the summit pyramid of Shuksan, we scramble over steep rock on our way to the peak. When we get to the top, we find a stone ledge big enough to sit on; this sharp summit is the size of a small room. I look over to Eldorado Peak, which I climbed a few days ago. I can still feel the height of the knife's edge of that summit, the sheer drop on both sides of an icy pinnacle.

Even though I was born on this land, I am only beginning to understand the depth of all that it encompasses and my place in it. Perhaps it takes proximity, measured with every scramble and footstep, to understand the space between peaks, instead of seeing them only from the valleys below.

I've traveled all over the world and come back to the place where I was born in order to make a home as my authentic self. I've found just that among a diverse and vibrant community of people, rooted in an astonishing natural world. With self-knowledge and acceptance, I've come to care ever more greatly for these mountains, the valleys of the Pacific Northwest, and the salt waters of the Salish Sea, for this earth beneath my feet. This land that holds me in the palm of its hand, protected and uplifted.

Kimmerer's wisdom returns to me again: "Becoming indigenous to a place means living as if your children's future matters." This philosophy girded me in the fight for equality; my work could mean that no one else would repeat what I went through. It gave me hope. It also felt like some kind of sacred duty.

There is more work to be done.

Back at the demolished dam, I'm feeling a new urge to see it from the viewpoint of the river. I make my way down an overgrown trail of dense slide alders. The thicket is dark. I snap and whistle to notify any predators of my presence.

I now understand why I was so struck by those two married men who lived five hundred years ago in North America. Before Cabeza de Vaca found them, they had never known judgment from anyone. The strangeness was not that they were married but that Cabeza de Vaca was there to observe them. His ideology was just as alien as he was. And yet he felt entitled to judge them.

There was a deep backstory for these married men—one more vital and vibrant than any label European people might try to apply. They probably met naturally, like our straight counterparts today, with no concern about what people might think. Perhaps they had been out hunting in the woods, or on a mountain peak, or out exploring their land. They could catch each other's eye and hold each other's gaze without shame. Their minds were not colonized, and their people weren't confined to reservations. They could move closer to each other, be a part of a mating dance as natural as their breath and just as vital. They could hold each other around the campfire without the threat that whole civilizations of men were determined to erase them.

They could make love in the open.

They could make a home together, without wondering if they would lose their jobs or be shunned by their families or jailed or killed because they were different. What a wonder their story is. Perhaps I can see it only now that I finally have the right to marry a man myself.

The account reminds me that there was a time when people like me were accepted as a natural part of society—as natural to this North American landscape as its Indigenous peoples. We have persisted, despite the many people and societal codes that have tried to force us toward dishonor and death. We have dignity and worth. And now, across the expanse of half a millennium, I know I am not alone.

Soon I exit the darkness and walk out onto the banks of the Elwha, in a space that not long ago was under water. For a time, this area was the lakebed of Lake Mills; today it is a virgin forest. I can see mature growth above me—a sharp line of pine that marks the former lakeshore. Below that line, the bright green growth of new plant life stands where the stagnant water once was.

The salmon have returned, and with them, seabirds and bears. So much had been lost because of the dam; so much has returned with the freedom of moving water.

A river, like love, was not meant to be dammed. It was meant to flow. Here, and in our society, man-made obstacles have been removed. In the aftermath, so much has grown in its place. Life fills the spaces that were once flooded.

My life is a part of this renewal.

This deepens my love for the land, and my life. The more I love them, the more I want to protect them. Don't we all seek to feel that connection, at home in our nature? In a time of often ominous news, I am bolstered by the knowledge that man-made obstacles have been removed in my lifetime, and that in the aftermath of their removal, growth and change may flourish. In this absent-minded reverie, I look down at my hands, raised to my heart in a kind of prayerful awe. My right fingertips rotate the silver band that sits lightly around the index finger of my left hand. I take it off and use it as a monocle to gaze beyond the river and through the open gates of possibility.

Acknowledgments

Throughout this book I've detailed a range of pivotal friends, allies, and family I've lived alongside, with literary inspirations from history, but many more people in my orbit have had a profound impact on my life and writing who didn't make it into this work.

To the allies I've met on this journey, from the sailors in the Navy to the firefighters I've served with, and all those I've had the pleasure of adventuring outside with, thank you for having my back.

To my first readers, Silver Galloway and Megan Grembowski, I could never have gotten to this point without your unwavering support through all these countless drafts. Thank you for believing in this story, and in me. And to my dear friend John Bailey, thank you for teaching me that we spend much of our lives coming into our authenticity, so we should allow others time on their own journey. To my siblings, Melissa and Josiah, you exemplify steadfast love and humble devotion, traits I've hoped to reflect in this work.

To the editors who helped shape this book, I thank Nicole Hardy from Hugo House; Christopher Frizzelle from *The Stranger*; Sumanth Prabhaker, Tara Rae Miner, and Kathleen Yale from *Orion*; Ellen Bass and Debra Gwartney from Pacific

University; Casey Lyons, Shannon Davis, and Peter Moore from *Backpacker Magazine*; Sabine Bergman and Sivani Babu of *Hidden Compass*; Forrest King-Cortez and the editors of the Parks Stewardship Forum; and the editors at the *Seattle Times* opinion pages and *CutBank*.

To literary agent Ethan Bassoff, who named this book and helped me organize it into a compelling narrative, although we didn't continue the work together, I am grateful for your time and expertise.

To the whole team at Trinity University Press, thank you for believing in this book and for all your efforts to bring it to print. And crucially, to Tom Payton, you have my endless gratitude for giving my voice a place to be heard. After crafting this book for more than a decade, I put it on the shelf. You found it and reminded me that it was a story worth telling.

Lance Garland is a firefighter, outdoor enthusiast, and writer. He has written for *Outside*, *Travel & Leisure*, *Backpacker*, *Orion*, and other publications, and his work has appeared in the anthology *Earthly Love*. His honors include the Pathfinder Prize for uncovering the first queer climbing team in history, a fellowship at the Banff Center's Mountain Writing Residency, a Catalyst grant from the American Alpine Club, and inclusion in the *Best American Journalism* and *Best Backpacker Stories of All Time*. He lives in Washington state.

www.ingramcontent.com/pod-product-compliance
Lightning Source LLC
Jackson TN
JSHW080910210725
87904JS00001B/1

* 9 7 8 1 5 9 5 3 4 3 2 5 3 *